FAITH, HOPE
and
LOVE IN THE
EARTH

*Rescue Mission in the
Space-Time Continuum*

JOBAH

To order additional copies of this book, contact:
Bookwhip
1-855-339-3589
https://www.bookwhip.com

To our Cosmic Designer in Space and Time,
Our pained World....Planet Earth

Read the end notes, in the back
of the book First to substantiate
its being a Science Non-Fiction Memoir!

Intelligence Information

I maintain that the cosmic religious feeling is the strongest and noblest motive for scientific research.

—*Ideas and Opinions*, Dr. A. Einstein, 1954

And they took him and brought him to the court of Mars' Hill saying: May we know what these new thoughts are all about that you expound upon? For you bring strange things to our ears: we would know what they mean. Then Paul stood in the midst of Mars' Hill and said: You men of Athens are too superstitious, for as I passed by I beheld the gods that you worship and found an altar with this inscription: to the unknown god—whom you ignorantly worship ... him, declare I unto you.-Acts 17:19-23-Mars' Hill, The highest Court in Athens also known as the court of Areopagites

The issue today is the same as it has been throughout all history, whether man shall be allowed to govern himself or be ruled by a small elite.

—Thomas Jefferson

INTRODUCTION

Dr. Albert Einstein said it so well that the "The cosmic religious feeling is the strongest and noblest motive for scientific research." I have written my literary piece as an observer of myself because when I look out into the stars and think about what I have been through in time and the spaces I have occupied, life tells me it is good when you learn that there is more to life than just what we see with our eyes!

Maintaining a good learning program and living according to health-based principles, one can think more clearly and actually do more. Someone once said to me that the word *Bible* is an acrostic for Basic Instruction Before Leaving Earth, and because I have learned that Earth is a completely contained recycling environment, my love of learning has afforded me direction and peace of mind and I know I am loved in the cosmos. Journey with me … Jobah is a female type of Job in the Old Testament. These vignettes cover six decades! May they bring you joy in the realization that your life is special and to be lived as a daring adventure. In the grocery store of time and space, one's choices and commitments make a big difference in one's quality of life. Reading and learning, over a lifetime is key, not only to sanity but to an eternal future!

CHAPTER 1

Between stimulus and response there is a space.
In that space is our power to choose our response.
In our response lies our growth and our freedom.
—Viktor Frankl

As Jobah looked out the main port window, off in the distance she could see the beauty of the Milky Way Galaxy glimmering with its multitudinous package of stars in its spiraled form. It looked like the sparkling effect that the sun produces as it hits the open ocean on a calm day. How calm it was except for the enigma of the cosmos's one place of laser spaceship misery. A majority of inhabitants, through illiteracy and superstition, did not realize that quarks, love particles, and dark matter all play a role in the Creator keeping tabs on their individual character development. Through the plans of the Creator, mankind had the design pattern for living the words of the Great Physician.

Jobah had been called in strict secrecy by the "Known's" highest command to be at project " TAV-Omega Shells" planning.[1]

Jobah wrote a poem in 1976 off one of the Ten Thousand Islands off the west coast of Florida. She explains, "I was crawling along the seashore collecting little shells called 'baby slippers.' They were a source of inspiration to me. The baby foot imprinted on each shell reminded me of each baby born and their shell bodies!"

> *A SHELL,*
> *Contains a lot of beauty,*
> *In its uniformity, design, and symmetry,*
> *A total uniqueness in time and space,*
> *Created by HIM,*
> *Like you and me ...*
> *Each shell bearing the marks of its DNA life,*
> *Under the sea,*
> *On its outward appearance,*
> *And yet on the inside, we hear,*
> *Distinctly, THE CALLING,*
> *To listen carefully is discerned the echo of ETERNITY!*

They all stared at the Milky Way Galaxy out the holographic-transmission port window.

He spoke:

"In Earth, they, with their lack of information, cling to traditions rather than historical scientific truth; matter, energy, and information make up their reality. They perceive the world to have three dimensions, little realizing the holographic nature to their existence. From camera-like eyes, sonar-device ears, and a high-speed data-processor brain system down to their perpetual pump-heart and incredible furnace system, their stomachs and boom elbows, and, of course, crane hands, they persist in using and abusing themselves and each other rather than thriving on information to build up systems all around them.

"Some realize that time stops registering its flow when *love* is exhibited, enough to shake existence and loosen its hold of unreasonable guilt and shame on humanity.

"Each must be put through the refining process. Each Tav-shell will experience maximum tragedy. Some more than others; their DNA code has been changed through generations of abuse.[2]

Ultimately they will understand that it is the acidic lie of shame and guilt that produces their agony of spirit, which is generated by the prince of the power of the air. At all times we will keep track of you through our laser telemetry systems—the science and technology of automatic measurement and transmission of data by wire, radio, or other means from remote sources, as from space vehicles, to receiving stations for recording and analysis. *Biotelemetry* (or medical telemetry) involves the application of *telemetry* in the *medical* field to remotely monitor various *vital signs* of patients.

"As a Tav shell, you will light the candle in others' lives to bring about changes that will envelope the whole planet. The simplicity of *truth* will prevail!

"The problem is defining reality to babes suspended in their three-dimensional space-time holographic continuum. You realize, Jobah, that space and time sequencing is different there. Each increment of information will be channeled through you over periods of time. Your timeless message is to be indelibly imprinted across the visions of all who read it, see it, and remember it, that *love* and *truth* never die but persist from generation to generation.

"Gather the rays of light in learning as you travel the space-time continuum of the existence you are being given. Dr. Albert Einstein stated that "imagination is more important than knowledge."[3] Many lose their ability to dream. You'll see why! Remember, individuals are enlightened through knowledge, wisdom, and truth, faith, hope and LOVE!

"Individuals take for granted their life-support systems. Notice in this diagram their diaphragm, a muscle totally controlled by their command module brain system. At night they sleep (a visual of biodynamic sleep action is pulled into view), and their autonomic nervous system keeps them functioning.

"Only those who recognize the high-tech nature of their body systems have a better quality of life than what the majority take for granted. I would like you to look into the annals of their time systems on the telemetry micro-laser disc, and you'll notice that throughout their history, force has only bred bitterness, hatred, and reactions on a negative scale. Hunger and want ravage the earth, and infant mortality is frightful. No one knows who will set the flame first on the detonator that would bring nuclear annihilation to large numbers of their species; tribalism and greed, on a planetary scale will set the trigger for nuclear atrocities.

"A culture of death now pervades the planet, and gross greed leaves the poor hungry. This sector of Spaceship Earth wants to dominate its fuel systems, while another section seeks to dominate the breadbasket!

"Only the unbending will of each individual made *aware* is capable of setting in motion the forces required for the 'consummation.' We see the twilight deepening over their entire ecological-ego system. The fate of Spaceship Earth itself, the edifice of creative, appreciative thought, generated throughout countless generations of their collective mind—it is this of which we are so gravely concerned.

"A knowledge seeker in their annals of time actually recognized the 'mind' that is free from compromise, from veiled slaveries. This seeker said, 'Mind is no one's servitor. It is we who are the servitors of the mind.' The fruits of their collective genius over the centuries might well have made life carefree and happy for all aboard the ship, not just for the few. Many of their national boundaries have been stifled by racism and prejudice, and you have high-tech instruments of annihilation being given to this generation, which are as dangerous as a gun wielded by a toddler!

"Social media has allowed seventh-century barbarism to be seen all over the planet, with individuals being burned alive, children having their heads cut off, and women being subjugated as mere property for abuse. The irony is they have the books of Moses-Taurat, the Psalms-Zabur, and the Injeel-the gospels of the Hebrew Messiah YAHUSHA. (The concise encyclopedia of Islam, pg 72.) These learning books are not out front like the Quran.

"High-tech weaponry is most pernicious when it serves to destroy human life and the hard-won advance of individual freedom-based awareness. The abject servitude that aggression in destruction propagates is a falsehood for growth and development—yet few have the moral courage to resist it. So, what could be worse than to be compelled into action that the truehearted regard as heinous crimes? The mass hysteria that breeds it!"

CHAPTER 2

"The most beautiful thing we can
experience is the mysterious. It is the source
of all true art and science!"
—Dr. Albert Einstein

Glancing out the portal window, one could see the shimmering imagery of excellence in form and design; a concentric spiral off in the outer region of the Orion arm, planet Earth lay nestled in its family of orbs called the solar system. Such beauty, such sadness! Jobah translated, with several cryptic pieces of information implanted, "Be ready, hang on, watch, wait, endure, and pray; a truth conceived in *love* can never die."[4]

Hosea fell madly in love with Ahabah![5]

Hosea had dated a princess in Ceylon, but Ahabah was beyond any woman he had ever met. The perfect measurements of her body and unique spirit captivated his imagination, and in a dream he saw himself married to her.

Ahabah saw Hosea as a real catch; he was wealthy, so she thought, and handsome, as well as a US Marine who spoke French and Arabic and was a World War II hero who earned both the Silver and Bronze Stars for his military action in the Pacific front. His great-great-grandfather came over on the *Mayflower* as a Separatist Pilgrim to escape the suppression of the government at the time against wisdom, knowledge, and truth out of the Scriptures (the Bible). Abraham Fuller fought in the American Revolution, and he endowed Jobah with being a Daughter of the American Revolution.

After ten months a beautiful baby girl was born. Hosea said, "She is a little Queen so let's call her Hadassah after Queen Esther in the Old Testament!" Ahabah said, "No, I want to call her Mary!"

> When from the wearying war of life I seek
> Release, I look into my baby's face and
> There find peace.
> —Martha Foote Crow[6]

The lights were dramatic as Jobah came forth from the womb. The doctor checked the child over, and everything was all right—almost. Instead of a small soft spot on the top of the skull, this baby girl's brain was unprotected; there was too much brain matter for the skull development. Her entire head was thinly protected by skin. The doctor called it craniotabes.[7]

Dr. Willis said, "Ahabah, a traumatic head injury could be devastating to your baby girl. Our concern is hydrocephalus. You must protect her head until the bone plate develop fully."

"Thank you, Dr. Willis. I will do everything possible to keep her head protected."

Two days later, mother and child left the hospital with the doctor's orders—protect the child's head. Ahabah was keenly aware of the intelligence of her child from the start. Jobah's eyes were a deep greenish brown and so large! Her alertness was evident as she followed her mother's actions. Jobah hardly ever cried, and those piercing eyes followed everything that moved!

Thinking to herself, Ahabah wondered if this could be abnormal. Maybe she'd remain this docile and turn into a living vegetable from hydrocephalus. She had heard about this condition, where too much liquid is formed in the brain and it grows bigger and bigger, causing brain damage and other sensory damage to its victim. She quickly put this out of her head as she hoped for only the best to come to this very special child planned for by her and her timeless husband, Hosea.

Chief Warrant Officer Hosea was stationed at Camp Le Jeune, North Carolina, the Marine Corps base. His grandfather was a doctor of divinity. He always considered that there were no atheists in foxholes, and World War II action in the South Pacific left him a war hero for patriotism and bravery, earning both the Silver Star and the Bronze Star. His great-great-grandfather, Samuel Fuller, came over on the *Mayflower* as a Separatist Pilgrim.

Leaving the confines of the Marine Corps base, Hosea took his family one day to Onslow Beach, located along the beautiful North Carolina coastline. With the pristine sandy beach before them, Hosea and Ahabah watched as their two children played in the sand. Jobah, at nine months, was extremely petite, and with her large saucer-like eyes and walking at an early age, she attracted attention wherever she went!

A group of Marines had just come out of the water when a helicopter flew overhead. Jobah, not beyond hearing distance from this group, was heard to say heel-e-cop-ter—heel-e-copter, as she strutted toward them with fingers pointing at the whirlybird as it whisked its way inland.

Hosea quickly jumped up and moved swiftly toward the little enigma, now being pointed at, smiled at, and enjoyed by the youthful soldiers.

"Hi, little lady! You want to fly in one of those birdies?" "Soldier, how old is your little walking doll? She's so small for such a big word like helicopter."

"Oh, she'll be nine months old tomorrow!"

"Incredible; mine's still crawling on all fours! Looks like you've got a future child prodigy!"

"Well, she's a little wonder to us, and she's in the *Creator*'s hands,[8] with time to reveal her destiny!"

Ahabah was on her third child. Ishmael was a tough delivery, but what an adorable baby boy! He was so cute he could have been a Gerber baby model. Ishmael, in his early years, was like an unruly flood; and in older years, he was extremely unhappy. Still, he was unique and loved his dog Daisy and his Parakeet Sammy!

Ahabah had her hands full when it all began. Jobah fractured her right lower leg being only two and half. Playing around, like all children do, she came strutting through the living room with one of her dad's shoes on her right foot. She turned quickly as her year-older sister called her from behind the couch. Jobah's foot, on the thick carpeted rug, hit the TV stand as she whirled around to look toward Mary. She fell, and a great piercing shriek echoed throughout the whole house. Her mother quickly came in from the kitchen to see what was the matter.

The emergency room doors to the military hospital swung open as Ahabah came through carrying a crying child in her arms. Tied around her waist was a rope that held an elastic cord with Mary tied to it following Mama. Ishmael stayed with a neighbor friend at the base.

A young corpsman came over to assist her as she plodded along like a mother duck with a duckling.

One week after that, Jobah broke her arm and was taken in for another cast!

Two days later a social worker arrived; her ulterior motive in coming was to find out if Jobah was a child abuse case.

Because Ahabah smoked, at six months old Jobah developed double pneumonia and whooping cough. Little was known then about the adverse effects of secondhand smoking on children; compounding the problem was that the collagen within the connective tissue in Jobah's bones was also in her lung tissue. Hosea was called back from maneuvers, as to all appearances, she was dying! Hosea was a man of prayer, and he saw with his keen sense of the divine that imagination and prayer were previews to life's coming attractions; he saw this child as special and with a destiny![9]

Thus began the series of fractures that would totally change the form of Jobah's arms and legs. In one instance a doctor was cutting off one of her leg casts; he bore down too hard, and a loud terrifying scream came from the table.

The doctor calmly asked Ahabah, now pregnant with her fourth child, if she was okay.

He quickly got the cast off without waiting for a response from the mother, took a needle off his desk, and sedated Jobah.

"Would you please hold the skin together here, Ahabah, as I sew up her leg?" he asked.

Ahabah, of strong Irish-German descent, acted accordingly in aiding the doctor in his private office.

A crisis developed when Ahabah and Hosea were bombarded with varying opinions as to what Jobah's future would or could be according to different doctors. One expressed the opinion that she could be tied up and not break bones as much, but she'd probably end up a nut! Complementing this was, "Let her go, and she would quite possibly die young, but a little happier."[10]

"Oh, Hosea, what a cutie Peter is, our fourth child. I am so glad his delivery has been easy on me. They are all so adorable." "Time for bed, children." Hosea carried Jobah as the lead car in their nightly enjoyment of putting all to rest. Ahabah carried Peter and Mary, and Ishmael followed along as they sang, "Choo-choo train a-chugging at the station, choo-choo train a chugging all along!"… To Jobah's bed, with side railings, on to Mary's bed, Ishmael's bed, and finally Peter's crib!

After putting all the children to rest, they settled back and talked.

"We need to make some hard decisions, Ahabah. I still have several years before I retire from the military. I've made an appointment with the base's clinical psychologist so we can talk about our family dynamic and maybe get some direction with Jobah. You have quite the load on your hands with our four children!"

Dr. Anderson said, "You can't raise three able-bodied children with as bad off as this one will be. Why, with the children just engaging in playtime and Jobah's continuous breaking by way of her brothers and sister wrestling or tumbling with her, it's uncomfortable to think about all the stress and anxiety! With institutionalizing her she'll be cared for around the clock," he interjected.

"Thank you, Dr. Anderson. We have some tough decisions to make. It's not her fault she's different, and many highly creative individuals throughout history didn't have easy paths paved for themselves physically or mentally. Why, progress has never come through mediocrity, but through rugged, rocky paths, paved by the blood, sweat, and tears of the courageous and enduring," said Hosea, whose grandfather was a doctor of divinity. He himself knew that in the foxholes in war, or life, one's destiny is determined by one's perspective and purpose in time.

Hosea believed that the mightiest force in the cosmos for the individual was the power of Prayer! His degree of self-discipline went above and beyond the call of duty. His mind-set was: "We are what we repeatedly do; excellence therefore is not an act but a habit!"[11]

CHAPTER 3

The decision was made to have Jobah go stay with Ahabah's parents, Stephen and Deborah. Before that happened, the entire family, including the grandparents, took a boat ride on the *Andrea Doria* in 1956 to France. Hosea had converted to Catholicism to marry Ahabah, and they'd learned of a place called Lourdes, a place of healing, and they sure hoped for a miracle!

The *Andrea Doria* was a luxury liner; leaving New York, they voyaged across the Atlantic Ocean in first-class comfort. Ace bandages, along with casting material, were brought to care for any fractures incurred on the long journey. The parents had learned to set fractures. Twisted limbs developed quickly, yet they healed in their makeshift splints or half-casts.

The hope was that the faith of the parents, as well as that of the grandparents, along with bathing in some tubs of water, considered miraculous, would help. Jobah was placed in one of eight tubs and prayed for.

It was presumptuous, but if nothing else, it was hopeful. Hope is the mainstay of all that are aboard planet Earth. To some degree, hopeful dreams with prayer spark the imagination to the creative point—to act! Faith puts things together by assembling, ordering, and reordering all the elements in the invisible world as part of the Creator's handiwork for the development of each individual in the seeable world!

After traveling extensively to Nice, Paris, and the French Rivera, the family decided to leave. Stephen, the grandfather, insisted and rather than take the *Andrea Doria* back to America, they took an Italian luxury liner called the *Liberte*. Providentially, they were not on the *Andrea Doria*, which sank on its return voyage to the United States.

One night, halfway across the Atlantic Ocean, a squall developed that left many passengers aboard the *Liberte* seasick. Jobah was taken everywhere in a baby carriage. With pillows all around her, all thought, if jarred, she couldn't get hurt. During the afternoon of the sea storm, the grandmother was pushing the carriage from the dining area back to the cabins. The doors to the deck of the ship had just been swung open by a cabin mate, and out came several passengers. Ishmael and Mary were walking close to the carriage, with Grandma pushing; she lost her balance and let go for an instant.

The boat shifted, causing the carriage to move dramatically against a bulwark. Out the child went—hitting the deck! Grandma Deborah had the two children by their hands and let out a loud scream! Jobah sat up a little dazed and confused but unhurt; no broken bones this time. A miracle? On into the future, this child would experience many events that would leave family and friends wondering about her special uniqueness.

> Love is life,
> at an extremely high level,
> of awareness.

—Unknown

The first time Jobah received a distant message, it came through the eyes of a young physician, who had become a doctor rather than a priest. He expressed to her youthful mother that the child would be different and could be molded into any form physically, as gravity and pressure would continue to break her body and form her into a human pretzel. Dr. Jennings labeled her as having glass bones condition.

The child looked straight into his wide brown eyes, irradiant with the glow of a distant tomorrow. The strange bright light of awareness—that all would be okay—left the youngster with hope.[12] Crystallized in space forever was the memory of those peaceful eyes as he dropped his long lashes so she could not see more. He realized her depth and recognition of a shared secret to be passed on.[13]

Outside Dr. Jennings's office, in the slums of New York City, a taxi drove up and took mother and child on their way. Ahabah thought to herself, *why would such a knowledgeable doctor condescend to living in such as area as this?* It was an enigma to her mind, but not to Jobah's; she would be an instrument used in the hands of destiny.

Several weeks later Jobah broke her right lower leg; at the county hospital the parents were told that an immediate bone transplant would be needed to save her leg. Her grandfather was too old and her dad had malaria, so Ahabah gave part of her hip so Jobah's leg would not be amputated below the knee. Ahabah suffered the rest of her life with pain. She was a beautiful woman and dancer, and her life changed after that dual surgery.

Jobah was in the kitchen with Deborah, her grandmother, squishing pits out of cherries for cherry cobbler. Her mom, dad, brothers, and Mary were on the porch with her grandfather.

"Look, we'll call her weekly. For the next day or two, she'll be emotionally pained. Comfort her, Dad, and thanks for taking her in so the children don't break her body up ... children play—she has you now to play with and Mom," said Ahabah.

"We will keep in touch!" It was difficult for a four-year-old to understand those closest to her—her two brothers and older sister, and Mom and Dad—leaving her behind. As she heard her brother off in the distance says, "Bye, Grandpa," she crawled to the hallway and looked through the living room into the porch. Agony enraptured her mind as she screamed and crawled as quickly as possible toward the front door. Clinging to it, she wept. That night she cried herself to sleep.

> "Is there not a certain satisfaction in
> The fact that natural limits are set
> To the life of the individual, so that at
> Its conclusion it may appear as a work
> Of art?"
> —Dr. Albert Einstein

"I am the apple of your eye? Does that mean our eyes are made of apples, Gramps?"

"No, it just means that you are the most special person to me in the whole world!"

"What's the whole world?"

"It's made up of this house, the gardens outside, this city, this country, our entire planet! The big ball, the globe on the porch with all those bumps, big and little ones on it? Well, you and I live on a bigger ball just like that one," Gramps interjected.

"Let's eat dinner now; I'll answer more questions later!"

As they entered the kitchen, Grandma announced the delectables. "I hope you two are hungry. I've made mashed potatoes, gravy, steamed carrots, carrot salad, turkey baked in pineapple sauce, and hot apple pie a la mode!"

After dinner, when all was cleared from the table, Jobah was given a bath in the kitchen sink. She was uniquely tiny and fit in it like a toy doll.

Deborah insisted that the child go to bed early when she did. Jobah would crawl to a little floor bed at the foot of her grandparents' bed. A small board was placed by the bed's side so she wouldn't fall off the six inches to the floor and hurt herself. Everyone would say good night. and her grandfather would have Jobah recite, "Now I lay me down to sleep, I pray the Creator my soul to keep; if I should die before I wake, I pray thee, Abba, my soul to take."

Not more than twenty minutes after Deborah started to snore, Jobah would move the board next to her bed and out she'd crawl, leaving the dark room and snoring behind her. All lights would be out except for the iridescent glow of the TV in the living room beyond the hallway.

Stephen would be sitting at the hallway's entrance to the living room in his big wooden chair with armrests. Crawling over to his legs, she would cling to them, or she would be picked up by her Gramps with gentleness. They would smile at each other and stay up until two in the morning and would enjoy their togetherness and the images flashing across the screen.

On Saturday nights would be the fighting matches. There they would be watching Frazier fighting on TV, while drinking Budweiser Beer together and eating potato chips and her grandfather would talk to her about wisdom's secrets. (Stephen allowed her to drink beer and whisky for pain.)

"You must be like old Abe! Abraham Lincoln was a great and wise man. To be like him, you'll have to study hard and do what you learn, not just talk about what you learn. Too many people are a lot of hot air. You may be tiny, but you'll be mighty if you'll be like Abe and who he stood for. From a child and all his life, he had read the Scriptures (Bible). Jobah, you'll need to be a good reader; I will help you learn to read! Abe was firm for what is right!"

Stephen had raised his thirteen brothers and sisters during the depression years and had been a prize fighter as well as a street fighter. Where defense was necessary, he used his body, but he believed firmly in right over might. Having only an eighth-grade education, he had worked hard all his life. His favorite reading was the *Reader's Digest,* and he always read it from cover to cover monthly.

Having Hosea as her Dad gave Jobah insights into the spirituality of existence. As a warrior, Hosea fought for the USA during World War II which gave all, in America the freedoms we enjoy today.

In the Scriptures (Bible) there is an example of a Military man, a government official in King Herod's service. He walked twenty miles to ask the Savior (YAHUSHA), calling HIM Lord, to heal his son. This miracle happened over time and space....twenty miles distant! The SAVIOR said, "Go your way, thy son lives!" The Government Official believed and he obeyed by returning home....demonstrating his FAITH! The boy was healed when the SAVIOR spoke, thus demonstrating that distance was no problem because of HIS mastery over time and space. (John 4:51) Thus, the Government Official and his family became believers!

Like Hosea was a World War II hero, Stephen was a World War I hero. Recognizing the reality of there being more to life than just what we see, he believed in the brotherhood of all mankind and in being an asset wherever help was needed. Years later Jobah would think back on his persistence daily in saying she'd have to be like "Old Abe," and also his loving devotion in her being the "apple of his eye!"[14]

CHAPTER 4

———⚬⚬⚬⚬———

The day came when Jobah was to go back with the family. They were moving to a southern state for the warmth and Jobah's health. Variety Children's Hospital used a technique that would straighten bones. When Dr. Kaiser, the head of the orthopedic team, first saw the child, he thought she was a birth defect from thalidomide, a drug that caused ten thousand babies in Germany to be born with severe physical anomalies. Extensive surgeries were done. The upper and lower parts of her legs were broken in sometimes twelve segments, and a stainless steel rod was inserted to keep the bones straight; with living in casts up to her neck and almost dying through several of these surgeries to straighten her out physically, she remembers her childhood as severe pain, terror, and a lot of horror, but Jobah could finally sit in a wheelchair normally.

At twelve years old she purchased a Bible at Homestead Air Force Base for $2.00. The only book she read was the book of Revelation. In her art class she etched an image that was half-Greek in meaning and half Hebrew on the lion of the tribe of Judah. This etching ended up at the Union Carbide Exhibition Hall in New York City!

Jobah volunteered as a candy striper at the children's hospital where she had her surgeries; she loved to work with the children on the different wards. "Sandy, I have three selections for you today to choose from: *Horton the Elephant, Bambi,* or *The incredible Journey?*" After explaining the main characters in each book, Sandy decided to hear about the special elephant who always did what he said he would do.

The floor nurse finally came in to check Sandy's IV. At this stage of cancer therapy, the child had no hair on her head, and her arms and legs were so skinny that she looked like a skeleton. It was awesome to think that Sandy's body was being eaten up, and her own special defense system could not stop the invasion of this alien element. Her perpetual motion machine (her heart) would finally give way to failure.

The nurse asked Jobah to leave, and Sandy protested.

"I'll be back next Sunday, Sandy, and I'll have another good book to read, or maybe by then you'll be in a wheelchair like me, and we'll wheel to the playroom together, okay?"

Sandy looked so sad as she smiled.

"Remember Horton the Elephant's words: 'I said what I said and I said what I meant; an elephant's word is 100 percent'—and mine is too, Sandy. I'll see you in the future."

That next week Hurricane Donna flashed through the southern states, leaving a wake of destruction. Hosea had left his Weimaraner hunting dogs outside for a few minutes. Winds were still gusting up to forty miles per hour, so the palm trees' ferns along the driveway swayed with great vehemence.

Travis, the big gray, had zeroed in on a squirrel that had gotten itself into a real bind. As it tried to jump from one palm-tree fern to another, it miscalculated the wind and movement of the fern and hit the pavement in the road. Hosea was on the porch steps' calling for the dogs to come in when he saw what was going on. He got the dogs in the house, and then he went to get a shoe box to scoop the squirrel off the road.

"Dad, is the little creature still alive?"

"Yes, but I'll not have a diseased rodent in the house for you to take care of if that is what you're driving at."

"How do you know the little thing is diseased? Why, it only had an accident with getting from one place to another. Oh, please, Dad!" Jobah protested.

He was carting the box to the back junk area, and Jobah sped as fast as her wheels would carry her to the back ramp door.

"Look, Dad, let me take care of the squirrel. You can't just leave him out there alive, and there is still life and breath in the fluff ball." She finally talked him into letting her nurse the little creature.

"Okay, your name will be Horton!" For days she used an eyedropper for water and chewed up nuts and seeds, placing them into Horton's mouth from her own. For hours she mulled over the detail and beauty of Horton's body design.

The weekend after the big storm, Jobah went to see Sandy with some new books and her own story of Horton the Squirrel. Her mind went blank as she wheeled into an empty room. Sandy had died; she had been so cheerful through it all, and that last day looking into her eyes, Jobah saw such simple, trusting tranquility. How could this be? The world Sandy had lived in was so narrow, and now it had been cut short—in perspective, closed to the vast expanse of creative pleasures that most children enjoyed.

That afternoon at home, Mary had some of her girlfriends over. On her side of the room that she shared with Jobah, they were measuring their hips, waists, and breasts. As Jobah sat about fifteen feet away on the floor with all her art materials drawing, she thought ... *Where do I fit in?* It was hard growing up being different.

Jobah was a lover of books, and reading was one of her favorite pastimes. This particular day, while reading the *Snow Goose* by Paul Gallico, she sat alone, crying. The *Snow Goose* is a simple, short parable on the regenerative power of friendship and love. The Canada-bred wanderer of the airways had gotten shot, and a disabled hunchback, Philip, an artist living a solitary life in an abandoned lighthouse in the marshlands of Essex, cares for the goose; he also saves several hundred men with his little sailboat during the British retreat from Dunkirk. Philip dies in the process, but because of his body form and design, he was shunned by the community. The statement that overwhelmed Jobah was that deformity breeds a type of hatred in mankind. She never forgot that!

Horton was propelling himself across the living room floor as Jobah entered from the swimming pool area. It had been several weeks now since the accident. There had to be fractures! Only three legs were moving normally, so she called different vets asking them about their knowledge of squirrels, but none wanted to get involved.

Ahabah saw the pain in her daughter's countenance and ended up calling the Crandon Park Zoo vet. He said, "Bring the squirrel in!" A big-time zoo veterinarian that worked with lions, tigers, and bears told a total stranger to bring in a hurt squirrel. This vet had to be special!

Ahabah, Jobah, and Horton ended up at a beachfront residence in Key Biscayne, Florida. Out front was a black panther, with a silver and gold collar at least three inches thick around his neck, basking in the morning sun. When Dr. Scott came out and greeted them at their car, he appeared to be such a mild-mannered man. With great tenderness and sensitivity, he scanned Horton's body with his massive, masculine hands. With few words he said, "I'll call you in the next couple of days."

Sure enough, three days later he called to tell Jobah he had wired Horton's jaw on the left side together and had to refracture the creature's right hip area to set it correctly.

"Jobah, you did an excellent job in feeding the squirrel. We'll give Horton a couple of weeks to heal, and then would you like him back or would you prefer the squirrel becoming a zoo resident?"

"Definitely a zoo resident, Dr. Scott, as my dad's dogs might find opportunity to do adversity to Horton. Thank you for fixing the little creature's body up!" An imprint of integrity and compassion irradiated her mind as she considered Dr. Scott's sensitivity. Like a tidal wave of "joy," in awareness, she thought, "Truth and love are key issues in time's unending care for all living things.

CHAPTER 5

By age sixteen Jobah was having her artwork exhibited in several galleries and at different art fairs. Her parents had pushed her in this area of endeavor because they saw that as the world was, she would not be accepted in just any profession. With structural barriers due to her wheelchair and society's mores based on what was acceptable in different circles, she was a minority, a type of outcast. Medical science saw her as defective, and when it came to her family's activities, she was restricted; her siblings enjoyed active sports—swimming, tennis, football, and baseball.

"Dad, World Academy School for Foreign Studies accepted my portfolio, and I told them about my wheelchair. I'll get to travel in five different countries for my course of study. Isn't that great! Here, read the letter."

Her parents had their doubts about any airlines in the sixties taking her on a flight, let alone an international flight. Now, her art portfolio qualified her to study at the University of Florence, the Prado in Madrid, Spain, and the Louvre in Paris. Her parents' great trepidation came as a result of their own fears for her safety and well-being. What if she broke a bone? There were so many unknowns.

Nonetheless, Hosea and Ahabah decided to let her go. Their thoughts drifted to that early childhood physician who said, "Let her go, and she'll break up a storm, but she'll be happier if she lives!"

Jobah studied for three months on the countries she would be visiting, and with information condensed in one notebook, art supplies, several ace bandages, and some casting material in her suitcase, her TWA flight out of Kennedy International Airport was exciting. The exhilaration of takeoff and the beauty of cotton ball-shaped clouds out her airship window left her in awe as she contemplated the wonders of travel.

Her first trans-Atlantic adventure at age six was riding the waves of the Atlantic Ocean. Now, riding the waves of air thermals thirty-three thousand feet above the planet's surface, her thoughts were abruptly interrupted.

"Hi, my name is Michael. You're with the same international academy as me. I saw you check in at the airport. What's your name?"

"My name is Jobah!"

"How did your parents decide on your name … it's interesting to say the least."

"Dad had been reading the book of Job in the Old Testament and realized that everyone has problems in life, so had a boy been born, he would have been named Job; little did they realize what intensity would come out of my birth and the appropriateness of the "name," as the only child planned for. When Adam and Eve decided to know good and evil, they slam-dunked the whole genetic-DNA code, and so here I am under extremes but living life to the fullest!"

"Michael, have you heard of the theistic-existentialist Soren Kierkegaard? In his *Edifying Discourses* (pages 67–86), he endears himself to me by his wording on the book of Job, chapter one, verses 20–21.

Job here expounds on a principle of knowledge that down through each succeeding generation, an individual can take to heart, using him as a standard of integrity. Job guides the generations that listen."

"Quoting Soren, "If the generation sees only happy days and prosperous times, then Job faithfully goes with them. If, nevertheless, an individual, in his thoughts, experiences the terrible and is apprehensive because of his conception of what life may conceal of horror and distress, of the fact that no one knows when the hour of despair may strike, Job keeps faithfully by his side and comforts him, not as if he had thus suffered once and for all what he would never again have to endure, but he comforts him as one who witnesses that the terror is endured, the horror experienced, the battle of despair waged to the honor of the Creator, to his own salvation, to the profit and happiness of others.

In joyful days, in fortunate times, Job walks by the side of the race and guarantees it its happiness; he combats the apprehensive dream that some horror may suddenly befall an individual and have power to destroy him or her as its certain prey. Only the thoughtless individual could think Job should not accompany him or her, that Job's venerable name should not remind one of what he or she seeks to forget, that terror and anxiety exist in life. Kierkegaard's analysis of the present age uses terms that resemble but are not exactly coincident with Hegel's and Marx's theory of alienation. However, Kierkegaard expressly means that human beings are alienated from the Creator because they are living too much in the world. Individuals need to gain their souls from the world because their souls actually belong to the Creator. Kierkegaard had no interest in external battles as Karl Marx did. His concern is about the inner fight for faith.

So, there we have a guidepost down the stream of time to live life to the fullest!" concluded Jobah.

"I sense that Soren, who suffered, had insights the majority of individuals don't even consider. Why, with you still being in high school and me in college, we still have so much to live out.

27

John Donne, a poet-philosopher, spoke of the whole of mankind, you and me being parts of it, Jobah!"

He said, 'All mankind is of one author, and is one volume. When one man dies one chapter is not torn out of the book, but translated into a better language; and every chapter must be so translated; the Creator employs several translators; some pieces are translated by age, some by sickness, some by war, some by justice, but the Creator's hand is in every translation and his hand shall bind up the scattered leaves again for that library where every book shall lie open to one another.'- John Donne

"This is the same writer who wrote, 'No man is an island unto himself, found in John Donne's poem called, for whom the bell tolls!' What we are doing, Jobah, is comparing our notes in time by our life experiences. Now tell me... you've been looking out our airship window a long time; can you conceive of us being on a big spaceship, and we're one big happy family contained in this world? Well, not one big happy family, but nevertheless all together on missions in time?"

"Yes, I can. I will be going to this design school in Illinois, and Professor R. Buckminster Fuller, who teaches there, said that 'in reality, the sun, the earth, and the moon are nothing else than a most fantastically well-designed and programmed team of vehicles; one could say, we are Earthnauts, in inner space! Astronauts go into outer space, beyond Earth.'

"Michael, my inner space compound has been pretty sheltered, but now that I'm getting out more, and here even traveling on the international scene, I'm sure my perspectives will grow! I am excited about life; I recently read a quote by Anna Tedstrom, an Artist student in Vail, Colorado. She said, "Your life is a narrative in which you choose to be the protagonist or antagonist!"

As a type of Job, I choose to honor the Creator as his protagonist! This quote was on a bottle of Synergy, organic and raw Kombucha. Healthy eating and drinking makes all the difference in the world for healthy actions in time, she said!"

As a protagonist Jobah embodied the spirt of freedom...She flashed on another of her many experiences. Once, entering the novitiate period for becoming a Benedictine Nun she marveled that for 1500 years the nuns were not allowed to have the Scriptures in their personal possession. With her personal copy she read it from cover to cover in three months and went to the priest stating she would no longer call him father because the SAVIOR said, "Call no man your Father in earth......further, when I said, why do we keep Sunday holy when HE said HE is of the Sabbath; (Friday night sundown to Saturday night sundown); The priest got bright red faced, barred his teeth at her and missed hitting her in the face by two inches saying, "This is the way it is and you just believe it!" With Jobah's Dad, Hosea, raising her with freedom of conscious she thought "This is wrong!" Leaving the order she went on to study Hebrew and Greek and even went to Israel three times.

CHAPTER 6

Michael was a very special college student; he always extended his help to Jobah on this trip. She figured perhaps he must have known someone or had someone close to him that was physically challenged. The attitude of the majority of people toward physical problems is a type of standoff mentality.

Looking out the window, she scanned the horizon and the great cotton-ball ships that rode so peacefully by her, with the curvature of Earth evident in the distance. Her mind became transfixed ... all of a sudden she saw herself out there ... mind suspended, and with a state of no present time, she saw halls ... a vast hub of halls extending beyond her, with choices made for traveling each hall. Her choices were based on foundational information as housed in the Scriptures. Her mind flashed on Revelation 1:3. Blessed are they that read!

From one hallway came thoughts of doctors who devoted years to the study of physical problems and the relationships of cause and effect. The cause of a misguided gene producing the effect of, say, hemophilia—a free bleeder—or the cause of alcohol destroying certain genetic material within a fetus, producing the effect of an alcohol-syndrome baby. Without the knowledge of cause and effect, even the retarded or emotionally disturbed are stigmatized.

Other hallways had those who didn't read. Illiteracy and superstition kept them bound up, and they became suppressors of themselves and others with drugs, alcohol, and self-loathing pain—and more pain spread through iniquity, and the beat went on to the next generation.

Then there was the hallway of breaking out of time, those that rise above being different, who show compassion. They contribute a page in history triumphed with the progressive awareness of all of us being unique, supporting each other—like in play these children of the mind see mystery and excitement, from the mote in a sunbeam to the cuddly friendship of a puppy dog.

Jobah loved to imagine, and just now her mind thought from her enjoyment of reading:

"Imagine that an amazing messenger from our *Creator* blessed you on the day you were born.

"Welcome to Spaceship Earth, little one. You are starting out on your life mission. I want you to constantly remember that you are created in the *Creator's image* and you are *his* child. He has created this world for your benefit and for you to have a place to grow and develop your character.

"You will live your life one moment at a time. I bless you to appreciate and be grateful for life with every breath that you breathe. You will need to learn many things to make the most of your stay in Spaceship Earth. I want you to get off to a good start. So I bless you with four qualities. These four qualities will upgrade your self-talk when you learn to speak.

"I bless you with *joy*! Whenever you pray or read the Scriptures or study, do so with *joy*! *Joy* will make every spiritual word and action more elevated.

"I bless you with courage. Have the courage to fulfill your life's mission. Don't needlessly limit yourself with fear. I bless you to experience joy every time you do something you might fear.

"I bless you with love, love for our *Creator* and love for being kind to people and animals. Each word and act of kindness is another opportunity to experience more joy!

"I bless you with serenity. That will give you an inner calm and a clear mind to be able to think wisely and creatively.

"You will forget that you received this blessing living on planet Earth, but these benefits will always be with you when you bring them to your mind. Joy is a true measure of an individual's happiness in Spaceship Earth.

"Awesome Joy is available to someone who has a daily appreciation of the world or of the complexity of one's own body, brain, eyes, ears, hands, and feet.15

Jobah's body never functioned like that of an able-bodied individual, but her awe at what it could do amazed her. When she broke both her arms, she could write with her left foot!

Michael asked, "Jobah, wasn't R. Buckminster Fuller born deaf?"

"Yes, solitude and silence pervaded his life, but this created a strength, a wellspring of design insights that others have benefited from in time. Truly, Mr. Fuller's geodesic dome on American military radar systems throughout the planet aids against high winds. He offered a lot of insights into the dynamics of the geometry of living within our biosphere—our biological home: Earth!"

From the Prado Museum in Madrid, Spain, to the Louvre in Paris, France, the group of students shared a wealth of insights together. One professor at the University of Florence in Italy actually drew nothing but a shrimp for six months straight! He wanted to understand completely, from every angle of design detail, this little creature of the sea.

Time was irrelevant to him. Understanding and knowledge of the subject matter reigned supreme. This individual measured life from every perspective and came up with beautiful creations.

Age truly can never be measured in years, but only in closeness to or distance from life! He stayed young in mind by living vitally, connected to understanding and teaching what he had gained in experience.

Everyone called him Professor Shellease. Shell, because he had a love for the sea, its shells, and everything related to it, and "ease" because he was so easy to talk to and so slow, yet so consistent, in accomplishing everything he wanted to do. He took Jobah's group to Assisi, Italy, for study, work, and pleasure.

"I want Michael, Kathy, and Steve to play your guardian angels for pushing you around these streets and buildings. We'll meet for a picnic lunch near the crypt of St. Francis of Assisi," he told Jobah.

Wheeling the area where this great humanitarian had walked left Jobah with many questions. At lunch everyone talked about St. Francis of Assisi's uniqueness. He came from a very wealthy family and gave up everything that he might be an asset to his fellow humans. Animals, in uncanny ways, related to him. His spirit of giving and caring was a drawing element for centuries. "Here was a time traveler that never lost his significance!" said Shellease.

Step-by-step, in ascending the catacombs of history's pages, could be seen the life of a man, intensified by the awareness of the human condition. This "awareness," gave St. Francis the capacity for comforting others and appreciating the simple things; his mission of mercy was permanently imprinted upon the students' youthful minds.

CHAPTER 7

In Rome every student had a choice of either staying in a posh hotel or living in an austere monk's cell for the duration of study in this city of art and architecture. It turned out that the monastery and hotel were in walking distance from each other.

The gates of wrought iron swung open as the taxi pulled in to drop several students off at the monastic fortress. For being austere, the grounds were embellished with the most beautiful flowers, vines, and bushes. The whole place was made of rock, and each one had been cut and uniformly placed to create a structure that looked impregnable.

The room Jobah stayed in was very small. It had one closet, a desk table, and a window about ten feet up from the floor with bars on it. *How sad*, she thought, *that the light blues, whites, purples, and reds of the elegant flowers could not be seen out the monastery window. Perhaps it was so high up the wall for security purposes, but, again, how tragic to build a wall of stone to hide enchanted grace.*

With the echoes in the dark of the night, without a watch or a light, it was hard to tell if time was moving or standing still when confined in a fortress of stone.

There is no light where there is no space, and where there is no space, time cannot exist, except in the mind and consciousness of a brain that sequences events in a time-space frame. This brain, this masterful high-speed data processor, can create in three-dimensional photography memory traces that capture everything from depth, color, and form to the rich tapestries of emotions … suspended in a unique instant in time, crystallized memories hanging in thought space.

Jobah's mind spun with devotion for the Creator's design of her … with what was the reality of her mind's ability to function. Taking a blank computer disk and weighing it on a scale, it will weigh about 0.7 oz. She could spend hundreds of dollars and load the disk with over a million bytes of software, and yet it would still weigh 0.7 oz. *Software has no mass.* That disk containing information, like her body with her mind's recorded information, are each residents in a physical system. Housed within that system is all the software that can be transmitted through the airways … in speech communications, in actions, and in *the power of prayer* … Time is a physical property; it varies with mass, acceleration, and gravity. Therefore, since *software has no mass*, it has no time dimension of its own. The real her, the software in her brain, was spirit.

Sleeping with contentment she knew she was the apple of the Creator's eye … like all human beings that make use of their minds and actions for the goodness of up-building reality in the presence of the *Father* with what they've stored in their memory banks. We may not be denied the *presence of our holy infinite Father* because *his Son* came and said, "And all mine are thine, and thine are mine; and I AM glorified in them!" (John 17:10).

Jobah read a lot, and William Blake's quotation should have read "see *a* world in a grain of sand," not "see *the* world in a grain of sand"!

Shei imagine the world as a hologram, consistent with scientific thought, just a trick of light allowing a fully three-dimensional image to be recorded on a flat piece of space; our seemingly three-dimensional cosmos could be completely equivalent to alternative quantum fields and physical laws "painted" on a distant, vast surface, concerned not with fields, not even with space-time, but rather with *information exchange* among physical processes. The holographic and cosmic information bounds are far beyond the data storage capacities of any current technology.

In the semidarkness her mind was transfixed by a laser beam of cheerfulness; every atom making up her mind and body was made in the inside of a star, and in Spaceship Earth the conglomerate of all humans lived for fulfillment.

She awoke with an ardor of zealousness as the word *saint* came to her mind, and she knew the term simply meant an individual set aside in life for a profoundly good purpose, a *paragon* of kindness, honesty, and acumen realized through the annals of knowledge, wisdom, and truth, formed by the forces that make each of us who we choose to be with the perspectives and purpose we assume as our life's mission.

Civilizations have come and gone. Yet in the records sustained, it is always these men and women, working behind the scenes, that have aided in changing the course of human history for the better. Each of them had a pattern to follow, and each mirrored a reflection of whom they admired the most in time.

An uncultured baby's mind becomes modeled and carved through time's well-defined growth and development systems, based in thousands of days of experience, producing years of high-speed memory flashbacks, to define sometimes just one action.

The miracle of the free action of the human mind awed her as she contemplated the great thoughts and deeds developed by earth's inhabitants down the corridors of human history. Time showed that the appreciative creativity of giving human beings was instrumental in allowing another generation to come and go and keep the planet afloat. Forever realized in her mind was the reality that we come into the world naked and we go out that way as our spirit goes back to the Creator, who gave us the gift of life![16] Schedules were given each morning at breakfast for the day's activities: Breakfast 7:00 a.m. ... Study and work time 8:30 a.m. and so on.

At the beginning of each class-time session, students were given varied projects in drawing styles and in on-sight situations. Past projects included drawing masterpieces like Leonardo da Vinci's *Last Supper*. Jobah chose Botticelli's *Venus*, coming out of a shell, which she ink-sketched from the 1486 painting by Sandro Botticelli. Architectural wonders in Spain, France, Italy, Portugal, and Switzerland were included in the students' repertoires for their portfolios.

Today, all would draw from live models, nude men and women whose forms displayed the creative inspiration for all human technologies. From the delicate human fabric of skin, which in an average centimeter contains three feet of blood vessels for nourishment, to the articulate spine, which forms a column of solid cylinders capable of moving in any direction, to the intricate interaction of twenty-six bones, 107 ligaments, and nineteen muscles, coordinated to make the most highly evolved pattern of locomotion—the foot—all systems integrated produced beautiful forms for enjoying the world and adding to it.

In ignorance, the majority never learn the knowledge of the sciences to maintain these miraculous instruments of divine technology. Abuse of them over long periods of time causes debility, and needless suffering prevails.

Jobah's mind flashed into hospital rooms and old folks' homes, where the bodies of broken people with broken spirits sat around just waiting ... waiting! Going back to her early teens, her imagination transported her into the room she shared with Mary. Mary and her friends were measuring their waists, hips, and breasts. She sat on the floor at the other end of the room drawing pictures.

"June, my waist is 16, and my hips and bust are 32. What's yours, Kelly?"

"Huh? It looks like 34-16-32! With measurements similar to these, we could be models someday! Better yet, actresses!"

As they glanced toward Jobah, Mary said, "Remember, measurements don't make for true womanhood. I mean, ultimately, everything sags and crumbles with our bodies!"

The elegant, stately forms of the models holding hands before the students left Jobah with wonder as she considered these two human beings who looked like they could have stepped out of the Garden of Eden. They were perfectly structured in every way. "Well, Jobah, your keen eye for form, design, and spatial relationships leads me to believe that someday, with perseverance on your part, you could produce masterpieces in the art world! Professor Shellease eased his way around the students looking at each work of art, critiquing them.

"I would now leave each of you with a few words of simple wisdom. Reveal in your artwork nature's beauty, its intricacies, and try to capture the nobility of the human spirit—still present, amazingly enough, in a world seemingly bent on devaluing the individual and destroying itself. Create to bring enjoyment and pleasure, but also deep thoughts, to your viewers, and you will be compensated for inspiring them."

One night Michael, Kathy, Steve, Anna-Banana, and Jobah went to a nightclub. They had seen flamenco dancers in Madrid, Spain—what wonder, what sensual beauty in coordinated movements of men and women on the dance floor. Here they listened to loud music, drank beer, and watched as Anna-Banana and Steve were out on the dance floor gyrating to the beat. Michael sat there—contemplating the mechanics of the sink-in, sink-out effect of the strobe lights—and Kathy looked around, bored.

Kathy was a beautiful young college woman of Mayan-Spanish American descent. All the guys were afraid of her because it was rumored she was some type of underworld figure's daughter. She always dressed like a fox, and the way she wore her makeup, she looked a lot older than the sophomore in college that she was.

Out of nowhere Professor Shellease showed up! He sat down next to Jobah, and at first she didn't notice him due to her intense concentration on the project at hand.

"Well, Jobah, are you at it all the time?"

"Almost as much as you! Look at that drummer's side profile. Who does he remind you of?"

"He looks like Dr. Albert Einstein, with wild clothes on!" "Yup, that's what I thought. It's amazing, in the pool of humans' genetic makeup, down the stream of time, look-alikes can spring forth!"

"Here are some presents for you from our eternal city!" Shellease handed Jobah twelve long-stem roses, a beautiful Roman doll, and a big box of chocolate candies, along with a pound of Italian cheese.

"Why, thank you. I'm—I've never gotten—Well, I'm grateful for your kindness, and I'll never forget my times in Italy."

"You are a special young lady, Jobah. Keep up the great artwork. I must go now!"

Kathy's eyes almost jumped out of her head, and Michael's concentration now zeroed in on the large box of Swiss chocolates. "How I love it that you rate, Jobah," he said as he dashed a candy into his mouth after she'd opened the box to share with everyone.

"How do you rate?" asked Kathy.

"In all honesty, I'd say pity or patronizing, or just appreciation from one creative mind to another. I'm flattered, though."

"You should be … I haven't received anything but a pinch on the butt walking to class last week from an Italian macho-man." By now Steve and Anna were back, and they dove into the chocolates. "Let's go to the hotel and go over our portfolios before we leave tomorrow. Who's game, asked Michael?"

"All of us—let's go !" said Anna.

Michael pushed Jobah's wheelchair as they moved toward the center of the eternal city.

"Taxis pass this way. Let's wait here on this street corner a minute and flag one down," said Kathy.

Steve sat on the arm of Jobah's chair. His long hair came down a little past his shoulders.

A group of Italian men and women passed them, and one woman in the group threw money onto Jobah's lap! She became numb with shock at being considered a panhandler. Nothing like this had ever happened before. Little did she realize that in underdeveloped countries, like Syria or Iran, she would not have an education or be alive because individuals like herself were not treated well. In fact, they were looked at with disdain and given alms but no or little education; they were considered to be evil subjects born with problems.

Quickly she grabbed the coins and threw them back at the lady. With two beers in her, she became a spitfire and wasn't about to take any charity. She could look any age; with makeup on and her hair fixed up, she looked like a micro-Minnie lady in a wheelchair. It took Jobah years of Scripture study to learn humility and meekness.

"Ugh, how embarrassing," she blurted out. Everyone laughed. A taxi arrived, and off they went through the winding streets of Rome, with its wild drivers and practically no streetlights. "Jobah, do you want us to take you to the monastery now, or do you want to come up with us for a while?" asked Kathy.

"I'll come up a while and see all of your creations on paper," she said.

All of them were really hungry. Anna had a package of crackers, but Jobah had the cheese.

Jobah said, "Let's cut the cheese in chunks and put them in the metal ashtray and use that candle on the mantel to melt it!"

"Excellent idea, Jobah; you should take some design and engineering classes as you progress in your education!" said Michael.

Everyone ate cheese on crackers, looked over their drawings, and discussed what the future held for each of them in time. It grew late and the Swiss Air Flight left for Geneva, Switzerland, at 7:00 a.m., so two of the students accompanied Jobah back to the monastery.

Jobah's thoughts whirled around in her mind till all hours of the morning. Professor Shellease spoke words of wisdom, and his insights on life came from his life devoted to inspiring others. He often quoted others, and her mind was fixated on … *"Love is life at an extremely high level of awareness."* Had he realized her anguish within?

CHAPTER 8

Sitting by the baggage carousel with dark glasses and racing gloves at the Geneva Airport, Jobah was mentally considering how self-conscious she was, when her brief respite in thought was broken by a poignant awakening. A very dignified gentleman walked up to her with gloves and dark glasses and asked her in perfect French if this was the carousel for baggage coming in from Rome. Her dad had taught her French as he spoke it fluently from traveling every summer as a boy back and forth from the United States to Nice.

"Yes, this is the right carousel. I'm waiting for mine as well," she said.

"Will you be staying here in Geneva?" he asked.

"No; as I understand it, we will be staying at the Hotel d'Observatoire, in St. Cerque."

"Well, here's my piece of baggage!" As he reached for his leather suitcase, he continued to talk and asked Jobah if she would like a ride in his sports car up to the hotel.

"Oh, fun. May I bring several of my friends with us, as my chaperone would never allow me to travel alone in a new country?"

"Sure; I'll take you on the most scenic route up to the hotel!" With permission granted, Jobah said, "Steve, Michael, and Anna-Banana, this is Monsieur Damien!"

Monsieur Damien spoke broken English but could be understood. Everyone had lots of questions on his skills as a car racer. He exceeded the speed limit up the winding roads like a professional.

The van finally arrived with all the other students and group leaders from the airport. Monsieur Damien graciously dismissed himself, and the next bit of activity consisted of assigning the different rooms in the hotel to the different students.

The maitre d' of the hotel was calling out the different room numbers when he said, "Jobah, you will come with me please."

Her chaperone interrupted with, "She's with our group, and I thought you said we would be in one area together?"

"A slight change, madam! Jobah has the suite of the hotel, paid for by Monsieur Damien." "Huh?" the chaperone said. "Yes, she will come with me."

There was dead silence until Anna blurted out, "Heavy duty—the suite! Amazing how you rate."

"Come on over later, everyone," Jobah said.

In her younger years, Jobah would dream of flying and being free rather than being bound within the limitations of her own body. Another echo reverberated though her head. She realized that true limitations are only restrictions housed within the windmills of one's own mind. Sure, technological limitations would always exist because of her wheelchair and her inability to walk, but she could crawl fast!

She considered the lunar module landing on the moon. Like a baby, its mobility was limited greatly. Had Jobah lived on the moon, with its minimal gravity, she would have been five feet six inches tall! She was actually less than four feet tall. Gravity pulling on the fulcrums of her arms and legs at fifteen pounds per square inch was too much, so when extra stress was placed on her body, she would break bones.

From micro spinal fractures along one of the unique cylinders in her back to her vertebrae, fractured ribs, and so on, pain, immobility, and recovery time often left her with dreams of flight, which was a very normal reaction to confinement.

Just like a car that has become structurally overstressed because of a collision, the human body, as a tool for the mind's development, can be altered because of stress. The extremes she lived under, with structural limitations, could defeat or enhance her perspective. Jobah used her limitations in creative ways; she would just gather up the pieces and do something else within the space she had. When she broke her left arm, she learned to write with her right hand; when both arms were broken, she used her left foot to write.

So much mysterious wonder in the world left her always designing new perspectives and systems for coping—all based in the laws of physical and moral reality.

The Scriptures were her guidepost, and like a spaceship in outer space on a planet to be explored, her body-ship in inner earth space kept her busy analyzing and scrutinizing life. Many of her conclusions came by never giving up and praying or meditating for answers.

In time, she learned to fly an airplane with rudder pedal controls. Flying a Cessna Cardinal and a Cherokee 140 made her realize how aerodynamic principles are to be maintained for life itself, just like the Ten Commandments as exemplified by Christ himself. She gave up flying when she read where the Savior himself gave the relationship of Spaceship Earth to outer space.[17]

Meditating on *his* words in earth, she knew when flying out of Scottsdale Airport that she would give her bearings to the tower, and when she was landing, she would say, "Coming in at such and such a degree and such and such an altitude." Her mind focused on reality; everything was in and out, not up and down! Perspective and purpose were everything to her!

In her suite at the Hotel d'Observatoire, extending beyond her veranda, Jobah had a panoramic view of snowcapped mountains and beautiful Lake Geneva. Such an intensity of visual pleasure left her with the euphoria of peace, contentment, and deep thoughts.

After breakfast, they left their stone and timber villa and were off to the United Nations exhibition and a picnic lunch in the mountains.

So I walk on uplands unbounded, and
Know that there is hope for that
Which thou didst mold out of dust to
Have consort with things eternal!
—The Dead Sea Scrolls

High in the ubiquitous pine forest, all sat discussing the United Nations and the impregnable nature of this country engulfed by high mountains. Michael was chomping down on a peanut butter sandwich and drinking pineapple juice when he said, "Jobah, how about you going up the hillcrest with us after lunch?"

"I can't, Michael. It's too much to be carried up the side of a mountain. Why, you couldn't even see your feet in front of you!"

"Have you ever gone piggyback?"

"No."

"Come on and let's try to get you on my back, so you can be with us all."

"Oh, Michael, you're so nice in wanting my eyeballs to experience all the grandeur of this beautiful country, but you'd have much more fun running with the group. All of you go."

"No, you come with us!"

"Well, let's try the piggyback technique. Hmm, put me on the stump of that old tree over there. It has a good elevated seat level for me to slide onto your back."

The maneuver went well, and she was off for the first time riding amid the shoulder blades of a man. From youth she had recognized a deep-seated shudder, an aversion, a type of loathing some people had when confronted with even a slightly malformed human being. Her degree of intellectualism and sensitivity were affronted by this enigma. True, being different made her a spectacle, and people try to avoid things they don't understand. Her mind groped with these problems that separated this type of "untouchable" from the mainstream.

A hallway in her imagination appeared, a blue sky overhead, but her mind now narrowed by these strange hallways with their echoing thoughts. What was she hearing? Prejudice in race, color, and creed was so evident on the planet, but here was an even more deep-seated problem—this feeling of disgust felt toward someone different was developed, not acquired.

In the movie *E.T. the Extra-Terrestrial*, a twisted creature, misshapen, with big bug eyes, was the hero and friend to mankind. She thought if only each of us aboard Spaceship Earth could look on the others irrespective of race, color, form, or malady and care for one another as the miracle that each human being is … what a dynamic home or planet it would be.

Humanity's culture adapted from both creative and moral sources for advancement. Spanning time's corridors from Greece to the Italian Renaissance, some individuals with problems bucked the tide and came forth victors, with alternative ways of seeing the nature of reality. They thought, they observed, and they created by protecting their conscience through selfless service to mankind.

In America, James Madison, one of the signers of the Constitution, said, "Conscience is the most sacred of all property!" The heart of civilization has always been predicated upon the maintenance and improvement of culture.

Along with historical adaptation to improvement, moral adaptation had its roots in Judeo-Christian principles. It is in the

Judeo-Christian world that this *"heart"* has been more fully held dear … it respects the dignity of the individual for healing of the mind, soul, spirit, and body! In many countries the devaluing of the person is evident. Illiteracy and superstition pervade and the human spirit is often crushed.

Jobah's mind went back in time to 1970. She felt a calling to service and at twenty years old decided to become a Benedictine Nun. For the novitiate period of one year she went back and forth to get acclimated to the disciplines. 1971 was the first year in 1500 years they allowed the nuns in the orders to have the Scriptures (Bible) in their rooms.

As a protagonist Jobah embodied the spirt of freedom… With her personal copy of the Bible, she read it from cover to cover in three months and went to the priest stating she would no longer call him father because the SAVIOR said, "Call no man your Father in earth……further, when she said, why do we keep Sunday holy when HE said HE is of the Sabbath; (Friday night sundown to Saturday night sundown); The priest got bright red faced, barred his teeth at her and missed hitting her in the face by two inches saying, "This is the way it is and you just believe it!" With Jobah's Dad, Hosea, raising her with freedom of conscious she thought "this is wrong!" Leaving the order she went on to study Hebrew and Greek and even went to Israel three times.

CHAPTER 9

With her love of learning and reading, Jobah so appreciated current thoughts on humans' higher levels of thinking.18

This heart for improvement propelled her mind to consider how we were ever going to make it out there in space ... other worlds, friends to other beings, if we would propagate or continue the suppressive role of brute force or barbarism against our own species. Who would want the cancerous element that pervades the majority of earth dwellers ... the actual devaluing of the dignity of the human being or even a symbol of humans? Down syndrome individuals are simple in functionality but profound in their positions in time. The DNA code, their genes, makes them who they are, but they are so much more. Their different personalities endear them to those that love them!

Able-bodied men and women, given weapons in underdeveloped countries, suppressed by poverty and ignorance, armed to kill with instruments of destruction, use their bodies and commit suicide; this misery speaks loudly against our planet's cancer. All the necessary materials are available globally for training and developing each other's potential.

Ahabah, Jobah's mother, used to tell her, "Ignorance is bliss. Stop all this deep thinking, or you'll end up miserable!" But Jobah's mind would not let go of the knowledge of truth based in what is loving and beautiful.

Michael, Anna, and Steve were each one of a kind and treated Jobah as such. The smell of tall pines, the crisp fresh Swiss air, left all of them with memories shared that would last a lifetime. That day in the Swiss Alps, piggyback, with Michael and her friends, her mind again held consort with the eternal, the enduring universals of hope and faith. She was alive! A living, breathing, feeling human being, with heights to reach and be shared with those within her sphere of influence, wherever that influence would take her.

Nothing is a waste that makes a memory!
—Ned Rorem

Fifteen hundred miles away from home and one year after being in Europe had not dimmed that spark of excitement and adventure that swells within all at a new challenge. Here Jobah was, at the very university where R. Buckminster Fuller taught. Many of her classes were in the design department, and it was here that the thrill of creating and brainstorming new ideas flooded the air.

There was the bubble she could be suspended in to experience free fall in skydiving, and when the bubble-ball hit the ground, it would bounce without her shattering into a thousand pieces because of her bone condition.

Another one of her creations on paper—exceptionally executed drawings—was of a genetically engineered man of the future, whose expertise gave him webbed hands and feet. With Pilot man Helms Fish (as she called him) having sonar ears, as well as a lung system based on seals, he could dive to great depths and never experience the bends.

Earths inner biosphere—two thirds of it being water—could be explored by these high-tech instruments of humanity without the burden of a thousand-pound personal mini-submarine. It seemed idealistic at best, but how terrible such a tool as this type of engineering would be in the hands of a madman. Madmen have come and gone, like Hitler, whose regime experimented on handicapped children and in the end only proved that Aryan superiority cannot exist. There can be no superior race, as all peoples of all nations, of one blood, are in the same boat ship—planet Earth!

Another mind-bending idea was of the whole planet being a school, but she set the parameters of a literal school that would teach the basics but allow its students to travel the world and be a part of helping in underdeveloped countries in organic gardening projects and so on. If students wanted to learn the art of glass blowing, off to Venice they would go and learn from the best. Money would never be an obstacle.

World Game Theory, created by Mr. Bucky Fuller, looked so good on paper: everyone being sustained on the planet with food, clothing, and housing. All the nations and peoples of Earth contributing, up building, loving as one big happy family, each realizing each other's dreams. Anything that can be conceived in the minds of humans can come to pass. The big problem was how to keep each person and nation in orbit for growth and sharing. Jobah dreamed and loved her experiences in learning. Those were years of thoughtful integrity, but now how could she apply all of it to reality? Mr. Fuller's World Game didn't work when placed before the nations of Earth. So, what would?

CHAPTER 10

One of Jobah's major enjoyments was taking off on weekends, camping out and being filled with natural settings—flora and fauna in the wilds, sunrises, and sunsets. The spring before leaving Southern Illinois University, in the design department, her class was given an assignment: they were to design rafts to go from Big Spring, Missouri, all the way to the Arkansas Border, that being forty miles of adventure. Jobah's task was to sustain herself and travel those forty miles!

In Europe she had purchased a one-person pontoon raft. It was unique in that it had three blow-up parts—a base like mat-in inner tube within the main tubular form. It was made of a very lightweight material. She purchased kayak paddles and a life preserver and used her small Trans-World Airlines case for food supplies. She had rope, fishing lines, casting material, and ace bandages, along with a sleeping bag and tarp for the ground when she pulled up on shore. Her fellow classmates were there for her if she needed help along the river. With canoes tooling along and birds singing, she loved the great outdoors! Two gentlemen in a canoe rolled along Jobah's rig, and a conversation ensued.

John said, "You are a brave young lady to be in this neck of the woods; do you know what's up ahead?" "More of the river!"

Thomas, John's dad, said, "We have lived in these parts all our lives, and Goose-Neck Bend can be very treacherous for the best of individuals canoeing and swimming. How about you getting in our canoe and we'll pull your rig? It's only about a mile up ahead, and you sure keep up a good pace with your paddles, so we'll get there at the same time."

"Thomas and John, you know these waters and evidently have been here in times past, so you don't think I could make it alone?"

"Perhaps you could, but trust our judgment!" "Okay, let's go, guys!"

Rolling along after the transfer, they talked about everything under the sun. Father and son were both veterinarians out for some peace in beautiful scenery and to enjoy each other's vacation time. John was in his thirties and Thomas in his fifties.

The guys were amazed at Jobah's tenacity for adventure and independence. Now nineteen years old, with a severe disability, and she was out exploring over forty miles of a river in Missouri!

Goose-Neck Bend came upon them suddenly due to all their talking. The white river started billowing along the canoe side in ripples, but then within seconds, it looked like the white foam produced in a boiling caldron. With all their physical strength, these two men fought the twists and turns, ups and downs, boulders and tree stumps that were coming in front of them, pulling her pontoon all the while.

Adventure and thrilling experiences were her mainstay, and this bold journey made her mind soar with wild satisfaction; she was the *apple of the Creator's eye*! Knowing she was protected, part of her mission was to inspire and be inspired by the goodness of many. All life is reciprocity, and this was another adventure for her in the dynamics of living.

It was getting near dusk. The sun's brilliance was setting, producing a most glorious effect on this river in the Ozark plateau.

"How about camping by us?" John said.

"Okay! I have extra potatoes if you'd each like a baked one for dinner."

"Great; potatoes are one staple we didn't bring," said Thomas.

After nightfall settled, the evening's loveliness took over. The intense darkness produced in wilderness areas left the night sky illuminated with the brilliance of the Milky Way Galaxy stretching from one end of the sky to the other. Off in the distance, dogwood, oaks, and other hardwood trees cast a shadow, symmetrical in form, to a great big row of cabins, and the rippling sound of the river's moving water created a scenario of tranquility. Time is much like a river; one cannot touch the water twice because the flow that has moved on will never pass that way again! Jobah had taken several astronomy classes, so she explained the night's sky constellations and what planets were observable. With the warmth of the open fire, conversation lasted until late.

"Guys, do you sense that the cosmos is a digital simulation of a holographic nature? Everything has meaning, and like John Muir. said, 'When you try to take anything apart, you find it connected to everything else in the universe!" More on holography would come later in their conversation.

"My dad said the mightiest force in the cosmos is the power of prayer, and my experiences have allowed me to engage prayer and watch reality create what I pray for—like safety on this trip, and you two come along and get me through Goose-Neck Bend. In all honesty, with my degree of strength, I don't believe I could have made it alone! Thank you, guys!

"I've lived long enough to know that *he said*, 'Peace I leave you … my peace I give unto you, let not your heart (mind) be troubled, neither let it be afraid' (John 14:27), and voila, in *his* knowledge, wisdom and truth relationships appear, and all things work with precision and one has a better quality of life doing things the *Creator's* way!"[19]

John interjected, "I marvel at how *he* created different animals for different purposes; like the dog, for instance, a loyal and faithful companion that generates endorphins to an individual's brain when you pat them. What a healing generator of *joy*!" Have you had dogs in your life, Jobah?"

"Yes, growing up, for safety and friendship my dad got our family two German Weimaraners."

In the stories they shared, Jobah said she drove from Florida up to New Hampshire to paint the autumn leaves, and her Volkswagen Dasher became a magnet of attention when she would stop at rest stops or in state parks. It's interesting, the fondness that can develop when young animals are raised together. She found an Irish setter dying of severe malnutrition (got it back to health), a mourning dove that was brought to her when it was a chick, and on this trip, in the hills of Georgia, she found an abandoned kitten in an old barn … all playing passengers on this journey.

One other event she decided to talk about happened in Georgia State Park, Georgia. Jobah was not one to let people see her crawling on the ground, but this particular day she pulled into a campsite and decided to crawl down to the beautiful lake that was about two hundred feet away from the picnic table she parked her vehicle near. She scanned the area and couldn't see anyone or any campers. It was a Friday, late afternoon. Dovey always stayed in the Dasher; the kitten and dog followed her as she traversed some rocks and twigs with her skirt trailing behind her, carrying her Scriptures (the Bible).

"George, what is this world coming to? Look over there; a child is crawling, and an Irish setter dog and kitten are following her!" "You think that's unique! Look over at that green, four-door vehicle ... there is a dove flying around in it! Incredible!"

Because Jobah's wheelchair was parked next to the back door of the vehicle, George and Lisa didn't know until later, when they came over to her campsite, that she was physically challenged.

"Hi, I'm Lisa, and this is George; we wanted to come and visit. It looks like we are the only ones in this area of the park. It's so beautiful here. Where are you from, and where are you going with your wonderful family of animals?"

Jobah told them what her game plan was, and everyone enjoyed their time together.

The half-grown dove would sit on Jobah's head riding along the highways. In her mind she would be reciting all of Psalm 119, which has 176 verses; every eighth stanza is a Hebrew alphabet letter. Jobah was convinced that YAHUSHA had memorized this Psalm as a youngster; *HE*was so adept at navigating time, and that is what the verses deal with!

In the back window of the car was a bowl of water. Solomon, the kitten, would run around the bowl, with Dovey sometimes in the bowl flapping his wings. Lady, the Irish setter, had her own baby in Solomon and kept him clean in the backseat.

Animals, their behavior and habitats, and the Missouri flora and fauna left Jobah awed as Thomas and John told the secrets they had learned from their studies and practices as veterinarians. Their minds met as they shared their affinity to the great and small things on the Earth!

Looking up at the night sky and seeing the Milky Way Galaxy, Jobah stated in her enjoyment of learning that she considered that planet Earth was a digital simulation of holographic at its best! What we ask for, we receive! Of course, that is in the Creator's timing for our best experience. ("Therefore I say unto you, what things so-ever ye desire, when you pray, believe that you receive *them*, and you shall have *them*" [Matt. 21:22].)

"Jobah, you are more aware of the dynamics of reality because of all you have been through and what you allow your mind to study. Enjoying life taking care of animals and knowing that everything has meaning has kept me a very happy man," said Thomas.

"I'm still testing the wonders of prayer and time," John interjected. I was a pro-football star at one time, and in a game I was tackled and fractured my left upper arm and lower right leg. It was a nightmare navigating just the basics of everyday life, but my football prayer got me through it all. I'm hurt, I'm hurt, but I am not slain; I'll lay me down and bleed awhile, then rise and fight again!"

"Well, see you two gentlemen in the morning. Thank you for making my day safe and enjoyable!"

As Thomas and John saw Jobah crawl off to her campsite, many questions raced through their minds on her ability to cope with such striking odds against her. One thing was certain: she was making it, and she provided a unique event window of the human spirit's ability to transcend what would generally be considered insurmountable difficulties.

"Good morning, guys! I want to make the Arkansas border by 5:00 p.m. for my ride back to school, so I'm taking off early!"

The dawn was just breaking when Thomas and John rolled out of their sleeping bags.

There she sat near the water's edge, pushing her little pontoon boat into the water and quickly jumping in herself without getting wet. Everyone waved, and off she drifted, whistling the theme song to the *Sound of Music*. What reverberated in John's mind were the words from the song, "Follow every byway till you find your dream!"

The sun came up and brought everything to life along the water's banks. She saw bluebirds, turtles, white-tailed deer, cottontail rabbits, and beautiful cardinals flying across the river from one large tree to another. Time fleeted by as she moved into the future. One thing was dominant in her mind: with the aging process, she recognized herself as a passenger aboard the *Creator's* finest vessel, driven by the indwelling power of what the Scriptures called the Holy Comforter.

With miles of drifting, thoughts of great men, women, past experiences, and meaningful movies came into her mind. She loved poetry!

Ella Wheeler Wilcox wrote a poem called "Windows of the Soul." Part of the words came to her mind: "Let there be many windows in your soul that all the glory of the universe may beautify it ... and to the voice of nature, and your heart shall turn to truth and goodness as the plant turns to the sun. A thousand unseen hands reach down to help you (digital simulation—planet Earth—of a holographic nature, angelic beings helping humanity) to their peace-crowned heights and all the forces of the firmament shall fortify your strength. Be not afraid to thrust aside half-truths and grasp the whole!"[19]

Her mind drifted to the movie Star Wars and its number of computer-generated technological effects, even holographic images—precision-based manipulations of a given environment to excite the imagination! So, what are 256 special effects in *Star Wars* compared to the myriads that make up the whole of Spaceship Earth?[20]

Ralph Caplan said, "All art, and most knowledge, entails either seeing connections or making them!" (Ralph Caplan, born January 4, 1925, in Ambridge, Pennsylvania, is a design consultant, writer, and public speaker.)

Relationships were what Jobah's mind was keenly aware of and could define by way of given design principles under the laws of nature, the deep interplay of everything in the unseen and seen world—all given for the life-support systems of humankind! The word *physics* came from the Greek word for nature study.

Here she was 93 million miles from the closest star, the sun … being warmed by its rays, as she spun around on the largest of merry-go-rounds … planet Earth, spinning like a top at a speed of 66,000 miles per hour through the vast, limitless reaches of space. All systems worked in unison so she could enjoy the freedom of this beautiful nature setting, moving along with the current of immortal fragments of thought from special individuals that made a difference in what they thought about and acted upon.

Interesting that all the information based in the physical world came through the thoughtfulness of men and women who took the time to look and listen—physicists of the highest order—appreciative, creative, loving human beings who made ripples in time to benefit so many that they would never meet. Children's children all at play within one biosphere; campers in the stream of time, mining the rich ore that only solitude and silence relinquish.[21]

She remembered back to her arrival in Arizona, a warm, versatile state weather-wise. With its mountains and desert areas, she could choose any type of climate to be in within hours. Here was where she would work and play. After earning her master's degree in Education as a reading specialist, she would paint the reality of children and adults with reading problems. As a nurse or physician, she would administer the necessary piecemeal prescriptions to aid them in deciphering the code system that would allow them to read to learn!

Schools joys flooded her mind as she sat on the wooden planked porch of the one-room schoolhouse. Off in the distance she saw the blossoms on the apple and apricot trees bursting forth with brilliance, like the young minds that blossomed into maturity and developing potentials.

Ah, yes, to be set free from the bonds of the uninformed, not knowing where they stood, making choices for quality health, job careers, and good relationships. She as a catalyst would inspire their minds to the creative point to take action on their own behalf.

To know what to do with the bit of life each individual is given is to fulfill a need in Spaceship Earth, to be a part of making our planet a better place to live for everyone.

CHAPTER 11

———— ⌘ ————

The setting was grand for inspiring any person's mind to the creative point. In a scooped-out glen on 280 acres of semiarid desert property stood stone cabins and homes, as well as other frame buildings that served as classrooms and dwellings. Off in the distance were mountains and hills, which left Earthen Springs Institute, at 3,500 feet, a haven of beauty, with tall cottonwood trees and large Italian cypress trees around the main lodge.

Fifty acres of the property were tillable, so part of the curriculum for all residents, with both short- and long-term stays, consisted of gardening. To help those residents understand and be actively involved in the multidimensional curriculum, professional as well as paraprofessional individuals put together the dynamic of mind, body, and spirit workshops.

Jobah joined the unique staff of educators. Earthen Springs Institute was far from the ideals of any utopia—and in this world no place is perfect—but certain unprecedented qualities existed. Infinite kindness was tantamount to each person's progress through the programs they engaged in on a daily basis, and this is what the staff exemplified.

Paul Senior and his wife didn't have a vacation for eleven years, paying off the 280 acres for the retreat for individuals who wanted a better quality of life through healthful living based in the New Start Program. (NEW START = Nutrition, Exercise,

Water, Sunshine, Temperance or self-control in eating and so on, Air, Rest, and Trust in the *Creator*.)

Truly educated people are ones who have not only feelings of social responsibility toward their fellow humans, but also the intellectual drive and physical strength to engage in positive action within their community, country, and Spaceship Earth as a global village.

Two principal tasks were outlined at Earthen Springs Institute as keys to integrate the uniquely whole personality of each individual. Task one was to develop personal honesty and independence. Moral and social values were taught not only as pious formulas like, "You shall love your neighbor as yourself," but students went into real, on-sight situations to engage their awareness.

One teacher would let his beard grow for a week and then take several students with him to the Salvation Army. Looking like homeless people they would sit around and relate to the truly homeless; when a need was seen, these students and teacher would in every way create for the individual a special service or purchase what was needed to make the individual happy! The students were taught that a healthy social attitude is acquired though experience, and thus a collective spirit grew when it was practiced.

Intellectual development was spurred not only through the 3-Rs, but audiovisual stimulus recreated the past and present for students to understand their global historical roots. Again, on-sight experience was very important, and students were taken to special programs at local universities, junior colleges, hospitals, old folks' homes, observatories, places of business, and government complexes, as well as state courthouses and other countries, like Cambodia, to be aware of the real world in which they lived and their relationship to it.

Young, pliable minds saw the consequences of actions created through the lives of others. They saw debility in the courts where DWI's and bad health habits made wrecks of those who stopped dreaming, and strength in the lives of those who, after experiencing pain or grief, set about putting together a new design, a new pattern, a new use of the pieces from their efforts and that hope that was left them. Alcoholics Anonymous and other organizations started with individuals who wanted to make a difference, a new start for themselves, and be guideposts to others.

Mirrored in each life, when one took the time to listen was a unique story of coping, making life meaningful through reading and fulfilling experiences. When learning is fun, life is enjoyable! What about when one cannot read and life's experiences are continuously crushing? Cruelty may be removed from some people's experience, but it is the daily reality to others. The prince of the power of the air wreaks havoc among humanity!21

Wars, radical Islam, and satanic secret societies all wreak havoc globally. Now with nuclear weaponry, the Ebola virus, and other twisted biological systems to destroy mankind, everyone, through social media, the Internet, and travel, can be more fully aware of Spaceship Earth's global village dilemma.

> Do not pride yourself on the few men who,
> over the centuries have been born in your earth
> through no merits of yours. Reflect, rather on
> how you treated them at the time, and how you
> have followed their teachings!
> —Dr. Albert Einstein

He was born to set us all free 2,020 years ago now. Matthew 1:18 states that *he* is the Great Physician (physician = a student of nature). The *Oxford English Dictionary*, volume 7, pages 806–807 says, "A Physician is a healer. One who cures moral, spiritual or political maladies or infirmities. Inclusive in the term Physicists are the Anatomists, Naturalists, and Pharmacists." Jobah was now a part of this incredible team of educators emulating the instructions for health and happiness from the divine master.

Task two was to develop the physical prowess of each individual through the study of the natural and physical sciences, along with gardening. Jobah had a seventeen-row strawberry plot, and early in the morning she would crawl around and collect five big metal bowls of strawberries for each family and worker to make strawberry pancakes, smoothies, and so on for enjoyment and energy for the day.

Anatomy and physiology were taught as a basic in the curriculum from first grade on. Of all humankind's senses, it is vision that most acutely informs the mind. All students looked upon themselves as supersensory transmitter-receivers; therefore, if someone was of a different color, nationality, or handicapped, that person was not stereotyped in terms of being different, but in terms of transmitting what he or she knew from a different reference point. Consequently, such people were different only through one's perceptions of them.

Looking through the reference points of one another, they saw commonalities—namely, they were all in Spaceship Earth, studying the physics or nature of living for a better quality of life; looking through each other's eyes, they saw themselves in the brotherhood of all humankind.

With the teaching of general knowledge and the cultivation of special skills, the students' interests were stimulated not by competition, but by arousing a sense of pleasure in creative work. In the automotive department up by the shop, Jobah changed the points and oil in her Volkswagen Dasher. Two qualities are prerequisite for citizens living in a healthy society … critical minds and socially oriented attitudes.

This healthy perspective is the foundation behind Judeo-Christian ethics and the fortress that supports the dignity of the individual.

Jobah often questioned her mind; she didn't think fast—she thought slow—but she thought long periods of time on issues,seeing for an instant a re-creation of a past mission, a commission being recreated down the flowing ebb of time. A microscopic regrouping of elements would send forth thinkers and not mere reflectors of other people's thoughts; more special individuals would help in keeping planet Earth afloat for the consummation of all time through their experiences at Earthen Springs Institute!

CHAPTER 12

In vapid listlessness Julie leaned her head against the kitchen windowpane and stared like her mind was a million miles away. "Julie, it's lunchtime!" said Jobah. She had arrived that morning from the airport as a new student-patient of Dr. Rybursen. He was a medical doctor-surgeon-biochemist, as well as an exceptional humanitarian; adept in mechanics he also helped in maintaining all Earthen Springs's equipment, like their tractors. Between him and his simple, yet profound, wife, they kept on top of all the needs of the institute.

"After lunch, Julie, you can go for a walk to see the peacocks down by the stream, and at 2:00 p.m., Dr. Rybursen will meet with you!"

"This food stinks. What is this stuff?" she blurted out.

"Well, that is an oatmeal patty on a whole wheat sesame bun, with onions and homemade catsup. The food here is simple, but nourishing."

"It doesn't have any taste, and to think I am going to be here awhile!"

"You can leave anytime you choose, Julie. At least give it a try!"

All morning Jobah spent her time in the schoolroom, teaching reading or pacing the children in their varied subjects. At 1:00 p.m., she would go to lunch at the lower lodge, which had all the patients. This month there were several overweight people, one with high blood pressure, and Julie, who had come for rest and the warmth of the climate and to think about her priorities in life. She had not learned to read, and Jobah was challenged by this tall, auburn, blue-eyed, well-built woman. She had had several abortions, and one child she delivered was taken from her.

Jobah ate with the patients to be an encouragement to them in the lifestyle medicine program. She also lived there to help with the patients' needs. Every morning she was up at 6:00 a.m. and would have to go up the hallway through the kitchen to get to the bathroom that fit her wheelchair. Julie would come flying out of her room screaming and yelling four-letter words that she was making too much noise and did she have to get up so early?

Jobah answered, "Tame your language, lady. This is a place of healing, not wallowing in your misery!"

Over a three-year period, Julie—showing up during the spring season—made progress with her lifestyle, bad habits, and self-image, but what she put the staff through!

One day Julie was sitting on the couch at the lower lodge when the front door opened, and Jobah came wheeling in.

"Hi, Julie, how did your morning go?"

"Go? It went very slow—too slow. How can you be so happy constantly? If I looked like you, I'd kill myself; you're so twisted." "How can you be so miserable when, as an able-bodied woman with so much potential, you're so sad?"

Julie had tried several times to commit suicide before coming to the ranch. She was raised in a foster-care home.

All of us in life have such special backgrounds, special stories that make up our characters. Julie was bitter and terribly sad because of all the pent-up guilt and anxiety she felt over being left out, as well as because of her lack of love for herself. Julie and Jobah had something in common; whether one has been twisted inside by the elements of existence or on the outside, to support each other in all our challenges makes a difference! Julie and Jobah became very good friends.

Half of life and living to the maximum is missed by those who just go around making attempts only to understand the individuals they like or who like them. Many achievements of lasting value in history have come through the tragic lives of those who, with redirected energies, made a difference. Words from two thousand years ago reverberated in Jobah's mind, echoing their wisdom: "If you love them which love you, what reward have you? And if you salute your brethren only, what do you more than others?" (Matt. 5:46–47).

Julie ended up learning how to read; she also got her tubes tied after her last child was adopted into a family with four children. She went back to Hawaii and became a security guard. Through the years these two women kept in touch and would visit each other. The last communication received came by way of a mutual friend's letter: Julie had died from a brain tumor.

"Those to whom God has chosen to make known what is the wealth of the glory of this mystery among the nations, which is The Messiah, who is in you, the hope of our glory" (Col. 1:27, *Aramaic Bible in Plain English*).

Jobah, through time, recognized the constant, that living multidimensional gave one access to going back and forth in time. The law of self-sacrifice is the law of self-preservation; ergo, living through the event windows of others' lives in the present and living out loving others—to try to help them grow and develop— thrusts one along in the time stream in understanding the whole:

> Let there be many windows in your soul, that all the
> glory of the universe may beautify it!
> —Ella W. Wilcox

Every summer several groups of young people would show up to sleep under the stars in the back twenty-acre field. Two days of classroom instruction, with survival skills training, left the scouts with one night under the stars, and their two instructors sparking their imaginations with the thrill of future space travel and the wonders of interstellar space. Dr. Melbrook was a consultant to NASA and volunteered his time for Jobah's seminars.

Dr. Melbrook said, "Young'uns, if you're going to travel in outer space someday, you first have to learn all about your inner space environments.

"You get one body—a type of inner atmosphere spacesuit—and if you gum up your inner tubes, veins, arteries, and such through drugs, alcohol, or any element that impedes your command module—your brain—to think, it means you won't be able to function here or in outer space."

Dr. Melbrook continued, "As in Special Forces in the military, men and women who join the space program train now in lifestyle medicine for their future careers. Make your life's habits such that you can think and feel everything!"

Jobah knew well, from childhood, the overstimulation of drugs and educated the youth at Earthen Springs Institute to consider their health, based in the New Start Program, which was an acronym for Nutrition, Exercise, Water, Sunshine, Temperance or self-control, Air, Rest, and Trust in the *universal designer*. It was these elements that gave her, her great amount of energy and allowed her to function. She also knew that as one age, with a clear mind and a body that functions without pain, discernment of the invisible becomes more evident and profound. She thought of the power of prayer and what she meditated on coming to pass through the invisible holographic systems that the *Creator* designed into reality for all to experience life.

CHAPTER 13

Dr. Rybursen used the best in educational principles and medical technology to aid his patients and students in the care and nurturing of their bodies and minds. For drastic measures, wonder drugs and advanced systems, like positron-emission tomography for awareness, make a difference, but for them to be overused and abused is not good either.

Many individuals passed through the wrought iron gates that made up the entrance to Earthen Springs Institute. The Boy Scouts and Girl Scouts and other youth groups left their weekend retreats with farsightedness now encompassing their daily living experiences for their ultimate goals being fulfilled by their own choices made on a daily basis.

Jobah's mind flashed on a physic's *Today* article she read on April 19, 1981.[22]

It was nearing Thanksgiving time, and all students and lots of staff had gone to visit relatives or friends. Jobah was working on a computer program for instruction and decided to have a quiet holiday. Quiet? Never!

The telephone rang.

"Hi, Jobah. I have a request. My two grandsons are pulling in for the Thanksgiving weekend, and I've got a full house. Would there be a place at the institute for these two individuals for the weekend?"

"Sure; just give them instructions on how to get to the lower lodge. There is one room with two beds, and the brothers could stay there, and a private bath is in that section of the place."

"Jobah, they'll only be there for sleeping purposes, as all of us are getting together. You are invited to join our Thanksgiving Day dinner. Do come!"

"Thank you, but I have things to do this vacation time." "They should arrive tomorrow evening for the weekend.

Thank you!" said the vice president of the local bank. He had been a patient-student of Dr. Rybursen's for five weeks. He needed a bypass operation after sixty years of high fats and high cholesterol in his diet. With lifestyle medicine now behind him, his regimen of walking ten miles a day and eating simply left him happier and not having to be cut open.

Jobah got the guest room ready for her visitors. Extra towels were placed in their room. Things were spotlessly cleaned up, and she left a note: "Hi. I'm Jobah and will be in and out all weekend. Raid the icebox at anytime. Make yourselves at home. Enjoy your Thanksgiving vacation time in the great beauty of this area!"

> The creations of our mind should be a blessing
> and not a curse to humanity!
> —Dr. Albert Einstein

Jobah's mind remembered hearing off in the distance a door open and close that Friday night, but she just turned over in bed and hoped the visitors had turned off the porch floodlights for their grand entrance.

On Thanksgiving Day Jobah took a picnic lunch with her Irish setter and went off in the woods to think, pray, read, and swim. It was a beautiful sunny day, and peaceful respites in solitude left her rejuvenated for whatever the future held.

Behind every representation of humanity stood or sat much more than just the body a person inhabited. The global image was so infantile in its representations of what manhood and womanhood were all about, and a great deal of confusion about sex centered on the near-total concentration of the planet's mind on objectivity (what one looked like, whether male or female to perform sexually).

Except where psychology looked more fully on the subjective aspects of life and sex (and except for the instruction in different religions, grown vapid through the ages of lopsided advancements), models of awareness, based in the inward human experience, were few and far between. How many people were wise, understanding, and truly loving?

The hardheadedness that reigned supreme insisted that love, learning, wonder, womanhood, and manhood were youthful and beautiful. Marriage, fidelity, and grandmas were passé. The whole idea of the handicapped or aged being amorous or impassioned was regarded as disgusting! Some thought wisdom and love might be related or that perfection came through time and the study of both. So, much experimentation before study left the majority starved of spirit, and with a loss of life's meaning came self-destructive tendencies, a fear of old age, a ruined brain, and human sexuality being twisted rather than explored.

It was 2:00 a.m. when Jobah heard a call up the hallway. "Hello! Jobah, would you please come out so I can meet this ethereal woman that leaves notes around and is never seen? I will be leaving later this morning and would like to meet you before I go. I've heard a lot about you at our family's gathering!"

"Just a minute; I'll get myself organized to come out." Warren had told her a little about his grandsons. The older of the two was related to a very famous aviator and car racer called Eddie Rickenbacker.

When Jobah came out, she found standing by the woodstove a six-foot-five-inches-tall gentleman who looked like a large Paul Newman! As Jobah wheeled toward the woodstove, she noticed a bottle of whiskey sitting on the kitchen table. Because of her parents' alcohol problem while she was growing up, she was conscious of what alcohol can do to an individual's personality and ability to think clearly. She noticed that half the bottle was gone!

She said, "Hello! Your grandfather has told me how much he loves his grandsons. You must be very special." "You're beautiful!" "Huh? I've never seen myself as beautiful; I don't fit the mold, but unique and special for a purpose in time … yes! Will I get to meet your brother?"

"No, he decided he was going to stay in town tonight."

"I can't take cigarette smoke due to the collagen within the connective tissue of bones being also in my lungs; I am highly susceptible to pneumonia!"

"Ouch, I'm sorry, yes, I'll put it out!"

As a lifestyle medicine instructor, Jobah assisted Dr. Rybursen in classes on how to stop smoking and rid the body of nicotine toxins.

After much conversation about little things, their dialogue became more intense. By this time he was sitting on the floor by the woodstove to keep warm, and she was near him at eye level. He sure was a big drink of water!

Jobah said, "Half the agony of our existence is created by painful memories. It appears that by not seeing the Creator's restrictions as warnings about the plain facts of life, consequences ensue and misery sets in, such as alcohol dependence, but what is actually happening is destruction of the mind. Alcohol destroys brain cells, and the sixth commandment is you shall not kill. Altered perceptions are not good where true love is involved. I know it appears a lot easier to drown out feelings through imbibing, but science today knows that when you brine your brain, performance is depreciated!"

Jobah rolled up the sleeve to her right forearm. "This is seventy-five fractures! My arm is twisted severely due to a genetic anomaly. All of us are affected in our world, but we don't have to make problems worse through self-destruction!"

"That is grotesque. Your arm looks like a twisted pretzel!"

"Yes, I agree, my arm does look rather odd, but it functions.

I can write, and outside of holding a fork properly at the dinner table—and I always wear long-sleeved blouses—no one notices it unless I pull up my sleeve.

"Navigating time and space on a daily basis over a lifetime, one learns that the laws of *his cosmos* make a difference. Better incentives exist to do things right; not destroying ourselves or others brings happiness, peace, joy, and gladness to the mind, which is the heart. I marvel at my life of no pain now, even though I'm over 18,000 days old. Yes, I count the days! My childhood was extremely painful, but I live vitally connected through being involved ... happiness is a by-product of our efforts to live and help others to live as well."

"You mean you don't indulge in any vices?"

"What's a vice, but just a self-defeating action that ultimately creates pain? I was raised with some self-defeating behaviors, but always let them go due to my love of learning and what makes for the greatest degree of happiness, peace, and security in this world. We are all in circumstances where we can choose right or wrong actions; it's how we take the experience that makes us or leaves us in pained misery.

"I choose always to build up reality because *he said*, 'These things I have spoken unto you, that in me you might have peace. In the world you shall have tribulation: but be of good cheer; I have overcome the world' (John 16:33).

"You're something else," he said.

"No, I'm just another individual groping for meaning in life!"

"May I hold you in my arms?"

"Would you want to hold me in your arms if you were cold sober? You've had a few!"

"After relating to you, I've sobered up quickly. Seeing and hearing you makes me ashamed of being so totally out of it."

"You are right in what you are saying. The clutching fears and corroding hatreds of painful memories and addictions messing with your central nervous system will make a deep-feeling individual ashamed, and that's you!"

"I have to drive 1,600 miles today and I should get some sleep, but I won't go to sleep until you let me hold you in my arms!" "You do need to get some sleep; I'll help you relax, but to get involved with me sexually would be like a Great Dane trying to make it with a toy poodle, so please maintain yourself and don't try anything. Okay?"

When Jobah had descended to the floor and crawled over to the woodstove area, after he lay down, he wrapped his massive arms around her and tried to kiss her.

"Now, lay on your stomach, and I'll jump on your back and use pressure massage to help you relax." "And what will I give you in return?"

"Well, how about you try harder to stop doing things that hurt yourself and get into creating memories through your actions that you could live with?"

"Huh? That's easier said than done, you know!"

"Lie down now, okay!" She had never used a man as an object, for his body. Sure, she desired feelings of interaction, but not this way. It takes years of friendship to engage in a real dynamic of two minds, spirits, and then the icing on the cake—a physical relationship. Growing old together, and not cold together, was her idea of wedlock … the lock-hold of a vision shared.

He groaned and told her what a quality masseuse she was. Her elbows and knees worked with precision when pressure was applied. He experienced a warm flow of gentleness, safety, and a type of healthful wholeness through her hands; a pain within him had been lifted, filling him with peace.

Her garden work at the institute had developed her hands. Her fingers and wrists were dexterous and strong from weeding, planting, and digging. Soil—deep, rich, and lush—was her mainstay. She loved to watch beautiful flowers, rosebushes, vegetables, and strawberry plants put forth their fruits and beauty for others' enjoyment.

After a time it seemed like he drifted off to sleep. She mentally talked to the universal *Creator* about this special son of his and asked for help in his case. Jobah then crawled over to the couch and pulled the brown and gold afghan down to cover him with. As she neared his upper torso area, he rose up, smiled, and gently grabbed her.

"You're a neat man—a big, lovable teddy bear," she said. They embraced. He got as close as kissing her on her cheek. She kissed him back on his right eye—closed—and said, "Use this to see light and knowledge and watch always for lasting, happy memories in experience, to fill your special mind with. I must go now. Perhaps I'll see you again in the future!"

Jobah flashed on all the tragedies she had witnessed in the eyes of one that was despondent. Her life was one of service, which gave hope for the future. She realized we are made for trauma and tribulation, but *he* stated that in this world we could expect pain, but as *he* overcame the world, we would too by following *his* example on the physics of living responsibly or duty-bound. One day in future time, she knew, like a SEAL team six specialist, she would come before the commander of the cosmos, and she wanted the appellation, "'Well done, my good and faithful sister'

(John 17:10); you have been faithful over the things committed to you in your time of learning!"

She crawled over to her wheelchair, got in, and wheeled to her room. After an hour of study, Jobah wrote an inspiring letter on the universe and one's relationship to it.

He was rolled up like a big baby, sleeping soundly on the floor over by the big, warm woodstove. She placed on the table, next to his bottle of whiskey, the letter she had written to him. On the envelope she wrote, "Make it a happy day in your rebirth— another day of life in this time period called now!" She knew that some of the technologies she spoke about, like being in a digital simulation of a holographic nature, he would not initially understand, but ultimately all that love existence and question the elements of the philosophy of eternal life, as housed in the Scriptures (the Bible), come to realize that they are here by divine appointment.

Everything they had talked about she recapped in essence in her mind. She thought in these moments alone about the different men who had played up to her, including Philip, a handsome lawyer in his forties, whose twisted ideas of Christianity and Judaism led him to believe that one could be baptized by the Holy Spirit through the sexual experience.

Several proposals of marriage and the drives to fulfillment were there, but her conscientious nature would never allow using a man for his body or being used. Her fast sexually was a continual banquet.

The elements that matter in life are the things one does not do in the experience of true love's fulfillment. To her, the depth of love looks beyond mere appearances and is attracted by qualities alone.

She recognized the high-tech nature of the sexual experience. Considering that the most dynamic form of hydraulic engineering was a man's erection, she saw ignorance and abuse, through lack of knowledge and selfishness, as the propagator of many unwanted children.

If people would understand the body and its mechanisms and then anticipate the consequences of one's actions, overriding fleeting, momentary ecstasy, there would be less abuse of the system and more fulfilled true love experiences between men and women. Happiness to her was a by-product of living responsibly. Sure, there was cruelty—like the wealthy, handsome stockbroker who said he was very attracted to her, but the whole idea of going to bed with her grossed him out!

Men and women have multidimensional aspects to them, and where abuse, racism, prejudice, and suppression come into play, lack of compassion in thought, word, or deed ensues, and pain happens.

Each of our brains, housed within our body shells, is a fragile miracle of creative potential. As Winston Churchill said on October 29, 1941, "Never give in, never give in, never, never, never—in nothing, great or small, large or petty—never give in except to convictions of honor and good sense!"

Jobah saw the *Creator's* restrictions on her not as threats but as loving warnings about the plain facts of life and navigating time and space. The laws of *his* cosmos make it clear that wrongdoing toward others or the *Creator* has consequences. Incredible incentives exist to obey *his* laws of love, housed in the Scriptures..

One of the pains of existence for those who reject *him* is going mad. Tragedy exists all around us—rape, war, abuse out of control—so much of the world's evil is a result of individuals' failure to acknowledge *HIM* and do things the way *HE* said they should be done for a better quality of life. Being at the right place at the right time.

The Scriptures (Bible), blessed hope keeps one sane and at peace because *HE* has ultimate control and will one day step again into our time dimension and make us happier than we could ever imagine; being at the right place, at the right time involves more than serendipity... it is a miracle of physics...... ALL LIFE'S EXPERIENCES ARE BASED IN TECHNOLOGY BEYOND OUR COMPREHENSION. LOVE TRANSCENDING TIME and the spaces we occupy!

CHAPTER 14

———∞———

Taking a sandwich and some folders, Jobah took off to the office to finish the program she had started on the computer. It was May, and summer was already building up with heat. The tall cottonwood trees and streams around the property generated a good amount of humidity.

This particular summer she took care of three children, ages six, eight, and twelve years old. Jobah kept them busy with real-life projects. They had to go grocery shopping for foods they enjoyed and create recipes for the week's meals.

Reading was extremely important, and they read each morning and night. Gardening was a big part of their daily activities. They would weed and pick fresh vegetables for their salad each day. Workbooks were purchased for each of their grade levels so they would be on top of school starting in August. Finally, Mrs. Katz got out of the hospital and came to the institute to reunite with her children. Dr. Rybursen was really pleased with the outcome of her surgery and her drive to raise her three children alone.

"Jobah, I sure have appreciated your time and dedication to my children all summer long!"

"We really enjoyed each other's company, and I want to thank you for giving me the privilege of their care."

"Would you consider going to the Grand Canyon with us for several days of camping out and having such a spectacular view of the South Rim?" said Mrs. Katz.

"Hold on. Let me use my phone here to call Dr. Rybursen and see if anything is planned that I should be here for.... Okay, so with your invitation I will go to the Grand Canyon with you and your children!"

The doctor said, "Have a great time."

Mrs. Katz felt tired so she asked Jobah to take the children up to Yavapai Point to observe the South Rim in all its grandeur. She would lie down in the back of her station wagon and rest awhile. Jobah felt a little tired as well, so she let the children go into the museum and she went out to sit on the rock ledge. Getting out of her wheelchair and positioning herself comfortably, she noticed fifty feet down into the canyon a young man standing by the edge, looking over into the abyss. He was smoking a cigarette and started to scan the area around him and looked up her way. Because of the nature of the situation, Jobah immediately started to pray and meditate for the youthful man's situation. She had on a Korean coolie hat, and on occasion she would lift the hat to look into the man's eyes.

One of the children came out to say they were done in the museum, so Jobah directed them to go back to their mom's station wagon and she would join them as soon as she could.

After forty-five minutes the young man came out of the Grand Canyon; he knew he had to talk with her and she with him! He initially walked off, and she assumed everything was probably okay. Deciding to get into her chair, she started off back to the station wagon but decided to go back to the rim one more time.

There were juniper trees lined up, and as she got close to them, she saw Tomas, the young man, looking at her. Neither of them knew what to say, so she broke the silence and said as she picked a juniper berry, "Oh, look at this beautiful blue-reddish berry!"

He was from the East Coast and had one goal in mind: to see the Grand Canyon. Jobah asked enough questions so she knew he didn't need money or a ride or food, so she gave him the telephone number and address of Earthen Springs Institute and said, "If you come to this area, consider visiting one incredible place in time. It has gardens, orchards, and natural springs to enjoy—and individuals that are fun to be around!"

She went on to the station wagon and joined the family. They had a great time camping out and left the next morning.

Two days later a long distance collect call came, and Tomas said he needed help. Jobah called Dr. Rybursen and told him about the young man at the Grand Canyon needing help. The doctor said, "Put him in a cabin, but have him eat with a family with children." She drove 125 miles with a friend and picked Tomas up on Interstate 40, at Garland-Prairie road, west of Flagstaff.

Tomas fit right in; he quit smoking and got involved with projects on the grounds of Earthen Springs Institute. His high degree of creativity was appreciated. Jobah's mind was strongly attracted to his simplicity of spirit. He loved children and animals and, like the poet Thoreau, believed in voluntary austere living. A writer and poet himself, his endeavors in poetic imagery, landscaping, and carpentry never ended.

Nine months later he began work in Flagstaff, Arizona. His lifestyle medicine program took him to Country Life in Los Angeles and on to Seoul, Korea, where he taught English. Tomas wrote her from Korea. It was here that his faith plummeted into the furrows of all humanity being of one brotherhood.

When he came back to America, he worked with the physically challenged in Pennsylvania. Perception and awareness led him into his appreciation of Jobah's uniqueness. Transcending her physical being, he had seen before his very eyes the invisible manifestation of a uniquely beautiful woman in the varied ways she related to all within her sphere of influence.His intense mind often zeroed in on the essence of things as they really were. Within the realm of individuals, the majority of who they really are is contained in the invisible. Their body shells only project a mote of themselves. Truly, to judge a book by its cover was one maxim that interplayed here. He remembered a conversation he had with her on the schoolroom porch at the lower lodge. It was a beautiful sunny day and as he sat on the steps they talked. "Okay, Tomas, do you sense that what we do to build up reality, ourselves, and each other is recorded and kept as a record of our lives for an eternal future? Time's dimension never forgets!" "Let me say that meeting you at the Grand Canyon changed my life forever. For evil, good happened. I could have jumped over the edge of the canyon, but the edge of something greater drew me to continuance in life. I am thinking of a rather incredible event window on Joseph and his brothers in Genesis 42:21.23 You have exposed me to the idea of us being in a digital simulation of a holographic nature, and this substantiates the whole idea of what you do is recorded, and then over time, what is unleashed is goodness! So for good, evil happens. Joseph is sold into slavery but becomes the head of Egypt, and his brothers, needing food for the family, go to Egypt and they don't recognize their brother but he recognizes them! Time's dimension never forgets, and when one only does what is right, love stops time and happiness ensues. Joseph looked strong, proud, and very powerful and yet he was a reflection of the *Creator* in essence! His brothers resolved their evil actions."

Behind every event are countless previous events in an incalculable chain of time leading up to and causing the event to happen just as it does. And it is not only a chain of time but of space. Surrounding every event are countless other contributing events, countless interaction and confluences-a rain storm, heavy winds, random thoughts, the movement of the sun and stars, and the gravity of our Milky Way galaxy. They must all work together with absolute precision for any specific event to happen as it does and thus our prayers are answered in HIS TIMING!

"Tomas, YAHUSHA (the Hebrew Messiah) said, 'You shall know the truth and the truth will set you free!' In reading these sixty-six documents (the Bible's contents), it appears that the 'crushed bones' are an allegory pointing to afflictions; hence, the bones rejoicing paint a spiritual portrait of overcoming afflictions through *HIM* 'Make me to hear sounds of joy and gladness; let the bones you have crushed rejoice!' (Ps. 51:8).

"The *Creator* does not intervene in the hereditary slam-dunks of the DNA code and iniquity (absence of moral or spiritual values) being passed on to the next generation. We break iniquity by our choices, and the Scriptures (Bible) have been my guiding light!" Space and time are our friends if we follow HIS directives out of the Scriptures.

Space time is the secret structure that controls the COSMOS and this strange 4-dimensional substance controls time, light and energy as we bounce and bubble in the spaces we occupy!

CHAPTER 15

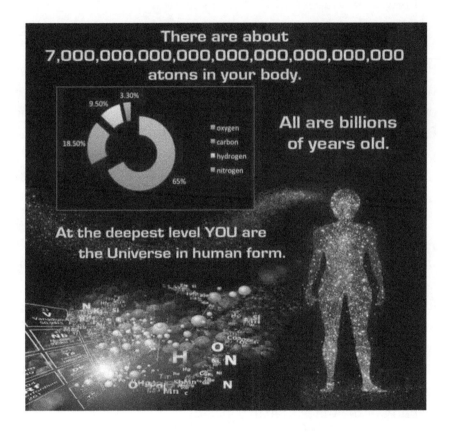

Jobah continued, "I found myself in the book of all time and so appreciated my existence more than I can tell you—knowing that my place in time, with all its troubles, breaking all the bones in my body, and so on, all of that has meaning, just like you and your travels. We are each so much more than what we look like! In John, chapter 17, *HE* talks about *HIS* relationship to *our infinite Father,* making you and I *his* brother and sister! Truly, at the deepest level we are the Universe in human form"

"We each have something to give in the annals of retrospective endeavors and actions now affecting the future!"

Jobah further commented on the diabolical nature in the world, where Islamic extremists remain hostile, as a culture of death, to the truths of the Judeo-Christian Savior and prey on Hebrew individuals and Christians as well.

"Persia is now Iran, and knowing the history, the language, and the culture lets us know who's leading in the caliphate of the death march globally. The prince of the power of the air! The robust *Savior of the world* gives us directives, and *he* promises one's *grace*-filled life will result in beauty, purpose, freedom, and faith, in the awareness of whom we are battling ... powers and principalities in high places, and only *he knows* what amount of this nightmare of forces plays out in the invisible world of ten or more dimensions![24]

"My life is clearly intended to explain and elucidate the practical realities of living in the light of *his* love and divine intervention. The invisible me is software housed within this body vehicle, which is hardware that can be seen and felt. Connecting the seen with the unseen world takes imagination, awareness, information, and knowledge. The personal miracle of my origin and mystery of my destiny lie in the strategic design of our *Creator,* who makes me happy by interacting in my life with *his* information systems. Truly, wisdom and knowledge are the stability of the times," Jobah concluded.

CHAPTER 16

Two days later, back at the institute, Jobah decided to go camping. Her mode of transportation was a three-wheel trike with an eleven horsepower Briggs & Stratton engine. It had two baskets in the back, where she would store all her provisions for sleeping out under the stars. Triple seat belting herself into her seat, which was eight inches off the ground, she sped off into the twilight hours aboard her chariot trike.

What was recapped in her brain at high speed, like a data processing machine, were the events that made her 24,000 days (Jobah's age in days) aboard Spaceship Earth worthwhile. Her "Grail-shelled" existence was torturous as her body shell took a lot; gravity was constantly pressuring and twisting this most singular vehicle—her body—which allowed her to touch the world and be a partaker as well in seeing, feeling, and being all she would present as her life's mission.

The hard-won advances of making others within her sphere of influence individually aware of their one short life spiraling out to others burned deep within her. The development of individuals and their creative potential, stimulated by the earth's collective mind, past and present, is the most valuable asset in time of one searching for meaning.[25]

The song so aptly goes, "We are the world ..." The fate of Earth and all the passengers aboard hinges upon its inhabitants ...

individual awareness. As Jobah had been a catalyst, others would go forth to affect the space-time continuum: students and schoolchildren of the mind—lovers at best—these behind-the-scenes players, unassuming ones who act out their parts in kindness, with every fiber of their intelligence and idealistic compassion for all.

There can be no fear-built security. The Hebrew word for fear is *Yare*; individuals who fear the *Creator* were considered faithful and trustworthy, for such fear constrained them to believe and act morally. Security is housed within our minds, and it's only as we use them for the now advancing technologies of astro-physics,[26] as well as electromagnetic and plasma disciplines, in realistic, loving ways, to build up and not tear down systems, that we'll achieve our destiny.

Looking out at the stars, Jobah realized that while traveling at 66,000 miles per hour through space, the Great Physician— the perfect *physicist*—gave directives that hinged on being aware of simplistic lessons of seed-sowing, nourishing a fig tree, and praying, always to be accounted worthy of seeing life for what it is … a miracle!

The Great Physician could ride in and out of the stream of time and actually change the molecular structure of individuals with conditions existing in the first century—leprosy, blindness, paralysis, and so on. That master of compassion talked of healing beyond the body, of awareness, of love for one's neighbor, of order out of chaos!

How did a routine recovery based in medical wonders today differ from *his* powers of instant healing? They differed only in the technology called vision and time. A miracle takes seconds; *he* spoke of regeneration … that change like the metamorphosis of a butterfly that would allow those that studied the physics of living to transcend time and space. Would it be possible to slip through the keyhole of the space-time continuum and escape the human concept of time? To ride in and out of life being a master of circumstances, rather than being crushed by them by being a victim in time?

> ## Must We Light a Candle to See the Sun?
>
> "Science and religion are not incompatible. While science tries to learn more about the creation, religion tries to learn more about the Creator. One cannot be exposed to the order and beauty of the cosmos without conceding there must be a divine intent behind it. Must we light a candle to see the sun? The more we understand the universe and the intricacies of its operation, the more sense we have to marvel at its Creator."
>
> —Dr. Werner von Braun

The *physician's* bright beams were reflected in each human being (shell) that she encountered in time; they acted as catalysts for her safety and peace of mind. All the special people! Thanks to cultural storage and transmission of knowledge, all human beings that read and study, stand on the shoulders of limitless giants to whom they owe their lives.

From the unique people of the past, housed in books, and books are like seeds, they can lie dormant for centuries and then blossom in the most unsuspecting human mind; to the dedicated young physician in inner-city New York who became a doctor to serve his fellow humans; to the places she traveled—like Assisi, Italy; to incredible humanitarians, like Dr. and Mrs. Rybursen ... all affected Jobah's existence.

Planet Earth was now at a crossroads in time; would existence now cease? Humans' minds' creations have not kept pace with their infantile emotional development, and, like children with terribly destructive toys, the attitude is: I want what I want. The Holocaust happened, and millions of Jews were exterminated as well as Christians; and now, full circle in time, extreme Islamic followers are working overtime to get full nuclear weapons technology and wipe whole countries off the maps of time.

As Jobah reached the plateau of the canyon, she saw a nice place to set up camp for the night. The sun was beginning to set off in the distance; like the miracle it was, this great plasma light-bulb set off such brilliance and radiance, it left her with more thoughts on the dynamics of existence.

Truly, technology is not bad, but neither is it neutral. Within the hands that control it, good or evil prevails.

Even the greatest of scientists and thinkers on earth today recognize that we are not masters of the cosmos. She saw herself and others as children to learn, suspended in a three-dimensional biosphere for growth and development.

Her learning experience left her with awe as a man, named Noah took 120 years to built a big boat, an ARK and at that point in history (space- time continuum), everything was destroyed.... drowned...except for Noah and his family on the ARK! Cultures all over the world substantiate this event in time.

Words her grandfather taught her years ago echoed in her mind just before closing her eyes for her night under the canopy of trillions of stars: "Now I lay me down to sleep. I pray the Creator my soul to keep. If I should die before I wake, I pray thee, Abba, my spirit to take!"

At 3:00 a.m., she was suddenly awakened ... Opening her eyes she saw a hallway extending from where she lay all the way into outer space. There, toward the constellation Orion's corridor, appeared an enormous light. She squinted, opened and closed her eyes, rubbed them, and still what appeared to be reality was outstretched before her.

W here am I going? Jobah wondered. In her wildest thoughts she imagined:

Like the astronauts pulling away from Earth's gravity to look at the beautiful blue orb ... planet Earth, suspended in space, a miraculous creation of intricate detail and design for humankind's development of each individual who wanted to learn. Information was the key, and she knew that back in the Earth, her mind and heart wanted all in her sphere of influence to be a part of this dream state! She remembered Sojourner Truth's statement, "I am not going to die, I am going home like a shooting star!"[27]

The imagery as defined in the Scriptures called the BLESSED HOPE, PREVATED HER THINKING: a city in space that could traverse the most dangerous of elements in cosmic space...... Black Holes are Regions in Outer Space that Intense Gravitational Forces are so Powerful that it Distorts and Warps Space itself. Black Holes Prevent Anything that Strays to Close to it to Escape!... Abraham, in the Old Testament desired a city whose builder and maker is the CREATOR OF US ALL MADE UP OF SEMI-PRECIOUS STONES LIKE Topaz and Amethysts as defined in chapter twenty-one of the last book of the Scriptures.

"And none can keep alive his own soul" (Ps, 22:20).

Semper Fidelis,
Jobah

My Websites:
ccisha.tripod.com
jobah.net
medicalmentalhealth.com

EPILOGUE

Now that you have been with me through the thick and thin of some of my experiences, I just want to add that, as Mark Twain said, "The two most important days of our lives are the day we were born and the day we discover why!" Adventures never end as long as one meditates, asks *HIM (OUR CREATOR)* for help when needed, and acts out one's convictions based in love and truth in the reality that presents itself to one with all the stimulus that never ends around us in our lifetime. "Terror and anxiety exist in life!" said Soren Kierkegaard.

THE ULTIMATE TERROR AND ANXIETY WILL BE MISSING AN INCREDIBLE FUTURE: Scriptural Texts: Hebrews 11:10, 16

If Earth still exists, which isn't likely since the sun is expected to swallow it in about 5 billion years. The best way to secure HIS eternal future is to accept the straight and narrow road…. Revelation 22:14-16.

The battle will continue for billions of years until the supermassive black holes at the center of each galaxy get close enough to merge.

The two galaxies will make quick work of one another. Just 250 million years after the collision, the remains will be a skeleton of what was once two independent galaxies.

Andromeda as it approaches the Milky Way through mutual gravitational attraction.

Right now, Andromeda is about 2.5 million light-years away. When it collides with our galaxy in less than 4 billion years, it will enter into a cataclysmic dance lasting billions of years that will rip it and the Milky Way apart to form a new galaxy.

Astronomers estimate that 3.75 billion years from now, Earth will be caught up amid the largest galactic event in our planet's history, when these two giant galaxies collide.

The Andromeda Galaxy is currently racing toward us at a speed of <u>250,000 mph</u>.

…CHOOSING HIS way out of what is coming: Book of Revelation chapter 21-22.

Painting reality on a daily basis can sometimes bring the mundane in with "Oh, no, another day," but the detail, texture, and tone of a period of time make the history of who we each are exciting and inspirational. I hope and pray I have done this for you! In the grocery store of time and space, one's choices and commitments make a big difference in one's quality of life. Loving to learn, history, science and technology, biographies and reading the Scriptures, over a lifetime is key not only to sanity but to an eternal future! Don't just live in your decades but read about the centuries and eras of millennia where men and woman have transcended their challenges mentally, physically and spiritually…life gives us exciting adventures, don't waste time!

END NOTES

1   Dr. Michael Denton, senior research fellow in human molecular genetics at the University of Otago in New Zealand, has concluded: "All evidence available in the biological sciences supports the core proposition ... that the Cosmos is a specially designed whole with life and mankind as its fundamental goal and purpose, a whole in which all facets of REALITY have their meaning and explanation in this central fact!" (From his book *Nature's Destiny: How the Laws of Biology Reveal Purpose in the Universe*, New York: Free Press, 1998), p. 389. We are in a perfect biosphere, with a war raging planetarily. It is a war of ideas, with their perspectives and purposes! TAV is the last letter of the Hebrew alphabet...OMEGA is the last letter of the Greek alphabet.

2   DNA is well-suited for biological *information* storage. The DNA backbone is resistant to cleavage, and both strands of the double-stranded structure store the same biological information.

3   Dr. Albert Einstein stated that "Imagination is more important than knowledge." Physicist born in Germany who formulated the special theory of relativity and the general theory of relativity; Einstein also proposed that light consists of discrete quantized bundles of energy (later called photons) (1879-1955) ()

4   Living in a digital simulation of a holographic nature, each gets what he or she lives out by his or her choices, perspectives, and chosen purpose.

      http://www.dailymail.co.uk/sciencetech/article-3057957/

Are-living-HOLOGRAM-time-scientists-prove-stra
nge-theory-true-realistic-models-universe.html#ixzz3ojWgFGpd
Read more: <http://www.dailymail.co.uk/sciencetech/>article
-3057957/Are-living-HOLOGRAM-time-scientists-prove-strange-
theory-true-realistic-models-universe.html#ixzz3on1llb7E

Arjun Bagchi, Rudranil Basu, Daniel Grumiller, Max Riegler.
Entanglement Entropy in Galilean Conformal Field Theories and
Flat Holography.

Physical Review Letters, 2015; 114 (11) DOI: 10.1103/PhysRevLett.
114.111602

Read more: <http://www.dailymail.co.uk/sciencetech/>article-
3057957/Are-living-HOLOGRAM-time-scientists-prove-strang
e-theory-true-realistic-models-universe.html#ixzz3ojZAOxcE

5 And Jacob served seven years for Rachel; and they seemed unto
him but a few days, for the love (Hebrew word is *ahabah, Genesis
29:20, love in Hebrew is Ahabah*) he had for her. (According to Dr.
Albert Einstein, "When a man sits with a pretty girl for an hour, it
seems like a minute. But let him sit on a hot stove for a minute, and
it's longer than any hour … that's relativity!")

6 Imagine that an amazing messenger from our *Creator* blessed you
on the day you were born. Imagine he said, "Welcome to Spaceship
Earth, little one. You are starting out on your life mission. I want
you to constantly remember that you are created in the *Creator's
image* and you are *his* child. He has created this world for your
benefit and for you to have a place to grow and develop your
character.

"You will live your life one moment at a time. I bless you to
appreciate and be grateful for life with every breath that you
breathe. You will need to learn many things to make the most of
your stay on earth. I want you to get off to a good start. So I bless
you with four qualities. These four qualities will upgrade your self-
talk when you learn to speak.

"I bless you with *joy*! Whenever you pray or read the Scriptures
or study, do so with *joy*! *Joy* will make every spiritual word and
action more elevated.

"I bless you with courage. Have the courage to fulfill your life's mission. Don't needlessly limit yourself with fear. I bless you to experience joy every time you do something you might fear.

"I bless you with love, love for our *Creator* and love for being kind to people and animals. Each word and act of kindness is another opportunity to experience more joy!

"I bless you with serenity. That will give you an inner calm and a clear mind to be able to think wisely and creatively.

"You will forget that you received this blessing living on planet earth, but these benefits will always be with you when you bring them to your mind."

(From *Life Is Now* by Rabbi Zelig Plishkin, City of Publication: Mesorah Publications, Ltd., Date of Publication, March 2010, Chapter 3, p. 24-25, Chapter 69, pg.227)

[7] Poem #31, "Peace." Martha Foote Crow, University of California Library, Berkely, May 6th, 1946 Craniotabes is a harmless finding in the newborn, unless it is associated with other problems, such as rickets and osteogenesis imperfecta (brittle bones) Science today knows that the DNA code can be altered through alcohol and drugs causing disabilities.

[8] "You made all the delicate parts of my body and knit me together in my mother's womb. Thank you for making me so wonderfully complex! Your workmanship is marvelous—how well I know it. You watched me as I was being formed in utter seclusion, as I was woven together in the dark of the womb. You saw me before I was born. Everyday of my life is recorded in your book. Every moment was laid out before a single day had passed. How precious are your thoughts about me Oh CREATOR. They cannot be numbered" (Psalm 139:13-17, p. 989, in the *Life Application Bible, New Living Translation*, 2004).

[9] Overriding reality the *Creator* sees the end from the beginning, and Jobah lived. No matter how suppressive the circumstances were, destiny played into divine design ... goodness happens!

[10] Peter was wild and wooly from the get-go, but aging turned him into a prince among humanity, whose mind and heart were strengthened by the Rock of Ages!

11 The Scriptures, sustained throughout the centuries, concur that meditation reverberates in reality, and with the waiting process, miracles can and do happen ... Hosea lived his prayers and came out of the war unscathed. He earned the Silver and Bronze Stars for bravery.

12 Helen Keller—blind, deaf, and challenged—made a difference in Jobah's life. She said in her book *Let Us Have Faith* (City of publication: Publisher, 1940): "Security is mostly a superstition. It doesn't exist in nature, nor do the children of men as a whole experience it. Avoiding danger in the long run is no safer than outright exposure. **Life is either a daring adventure or nothing!** To keep our faces toward change and behave like free spirits in the presence of fate is strength undefeatable!" We live in a world of trauma, and it's how we deal with the experiences that makes us or breaks us.

13 Matthew 18:10 (King James Bible, Cambridge Ed.) states: "Take heed that ye despise not one of these little ones; for I say unto you, That in heaven their angels do always behold the face of my Father which is in heaven."

The Aramaic Bible in Plain English (©2010) states: "Take heed that you do not despise one of these little ones, for I say to you that their Angels in Heaven do always see the face of my Father who is in Heaven."

We come into our world to develop character!

14 Deuteronomy 32:10–11 states: "He shielded him and cared for him; he guarded him as the apple of his eye, like an eagle that stirs up its nest and hovers over its young."

Psalm 17:8 states: "Keep me as the apple of your eye; hide me in the shadow of your wings."

Zechariah 2:8 (New International Version) states: "For this is what the Lord Almighty says: 'whoever touches you touches the apple of his eye—.'"

Theistic-existentialist Soren Kierkegaard, in his *Edifying Discourses* (pages 67–86), he expounds his wording on the book of Job, chapter one, verses 20–21.

ISSN 1393-614X *Minerva - An Internet Journal of Philosophy* Vol. 7 2003.

[15] *Life Is Now* by Professor Rabbi Plishkin, Chapter 3, pages 24–25, Chapter 69, page 227, March 2010.

[16] "Then shall the dust return to the earth as it was: and the spirit shall return to God who gave it" (Eccl. 12:7).

[17] "And he said unto them, When ye pray, say, Our Father which art in heaven, Hallowed be thy name. Thy kingdom come. Thy will be done, as IN heaven, so IN earth" (Luke 11:2 KJV).

[18] "A conception of person as possessing the self-conscious capacity to control one's own behavior, to make choices, to determine one's destiny, to love, to interact socially, to be responsible, to be competent— qualities that distinguish human existence as more than just being alive … qualities that are pertinent to decision- making in matters of life—at its beginnings and at its termination … derive their maturity from a biblical, Judeo-Christian way of looking at man."—Dr. Jack Provonsha, bioethician, *UPDATE*, Vol. 2, no. 1,pgs.3-7, January 1986, Loma Linda University, Loma Linda, California.

[19] Ella Wheeler Wilcox quote found at: www.poemhunter.com/ poem/ progress/ "I am giving you these instructions so you will enjoy a long life in the land of the CREATOR" (Deut. 4:40).

[20] "For you to be what you are involves a universe; and if your being what you are is the work of the CREATOR, then an infinity of events was under HIS hand. It was HIS skill to draw you out of the genetic pattern of your ancestry, the culture of your time, and the complex of relationships surrounding you. This is not to deny that had your ancestors been more temperate, your parents wiser, your teachers more conscientious and your school-fellows not such little beasts, you would not have been a better person than you are. Yet, such as you are, the CREATOR made you; and the supreme prerogative of the divine art is to draw good even from evil. Not a greater good, no; we do not help HIM to produce better things by offering HIM worse materials. But what HE makes is always a unique good. You are you, and no one just like you. The defects, as well as the advantages, of your background have gone into the composition of the mixture." — Austin Farrer (1904–1968). One of his closer friends was the Christian apologist C. S. Lewis; others included J. R. R. Tolkien and Dorothy Sayers.

21 "Wherein in time past ye walked according to the course of this world, according to the prince of the power of the air, the spirit that now works in the children of disobedience" (Eph. 2:2). "Be sober, be vigilant; because your adversary the devil, as a roaring lion, walks about, seeking whom he may devour" (1 Peter 5:8). "In whom the god of this world hath blinded the minds of them which believe not, lest the light of the glorious good news of Christ, who is the image of the CREATOR, should shine unto them" (2 Cor. 4:4)

22 "So the Ten Commandments and Sermon on the Mount are examples of cautifications: 1.The act, process, or result of arranging in a systematic form or code. 2. Law. The act, process, or result of stating the rules and principles applicable in a given legal order to one or more broad areas of life in this form of a code. The reducing of unwritten customs or case law to statutory form.

(Origin 1810–1820; code + -i- + -fication).

Of natural laws governing human beings that are in agreement with anything that has been established by authentic scientific investigation. So, does anyone debate that we ought to *love our neighbor as ourselves as a physical principle of reality?*

23 23 to preserve for you a remnant on earth and to save your lives by a great deliverance.[a] 8 "So then, it was not you who sent me here, but YAHUAH (Hebrew name of the CREATOR). Genesis 50:20 New International Version (NIV) You intended to harm me, but HE intended it for good to accomplish what is now being done. "They said to one another, 'Surely we are being punished because of our brother. We saw how distressed he was when he pleaded with us for his life, but we would not listen; that's why this distress has come on us!" (Gen. 45:4–8, 4 Then Joseph said to his brothers, "Come close to me." When they had done so, he said, "I am your brother Joseph, the one you sold into Egypt! 5 And now, do not be distressed and do not be angry with yourselves for selling me here, because it was to save lives that God sent me ahead of you. 6 For two years now there has been famine in the land, and for the next five years there will be no plowing and reaping. 7 But God sent me ahead of you ne, the saving of many lives. He made me father to Pharaoh, lord of his entire household and ruler of all Egypt.

24 "For we do not wrestle against flesh and blood, but against the rulers, against the authorities, against the cosmic powers over this present darkness, against the spiritual forces of evil in the heavenly places" (Eph. 6:12).

25 There are many technology statements in the Scriptures that the average reader takes for granted: the idea that the earth is round (Isa. 40:22), the fact that the solar system migrates throughout the galaxy (Ps. 19:1–6), and the fact that space itself has properties that transcend our three-dimensional understanding of reality. The Bible anticipated many of the recent insights of modern medicine that are in stark contrast to the myths and superstitions of the ancient cultures of the past.

"The very notion of a message from outside our time domain requires an understanding of the nature of our reality itself. What may be a surprise to many is that the more you know about the frontiers of modern science, quantum mechanics, and astrophysics, the more remarkable the creation account in Genesis appears." What Dr. Missler has done in his book 20/20 is bring into focus the future through the lens of Scripture. —Dr. Chuck Missler Prophecy 20/20 quote.

26 Astrophysics, Engineers are encouraged to think outside of the conventional x-ray industry and draw on emerging technologies from all disciplines, including computer science and medical imaging, and discover ways to apply new world ingenuity to the x-ray product. Astrophysics' engineering team has been responsible for numerous industry breakthroughs, including 6 Color Imaging, Remote Diagnostics.

27 Sojourner Truth is best known for her extemporaneous speech on racial inequalities, "Ain't I a Woman?" delivered at the Ohio Women's Rights Convention in 1851. Found:http://www.biography.com/people/ sojourner-truth-9511284

CPSIA information can be obtained
at www.ICGtesting.com
Printed in the USA
LVHW092045120120
643344LV00001B/4/P